WORTH LIVING

how God's wild love for you
makes you worthy

MARY DeMUTH

"With characteristic poetic grace, Mary DeMuth faces the question we all ask at some point: Am I worthy of love? It's an honest question layered with tension and fear, and Mary matches it head-on with her own angst and honesty. If you've ever struggled to believe God's love is for you—*you!*—you'll find both wise counsel and a compassionate friend in *Worth Living*."

Michele Cushatt, author of *Undone*

"Mary's beautiful, strong words are a healing balm to a desperate heart, a soothing song to a woman who has spent far too long doubting her true worth. A must-read for any woman who needs that tiny boost of inspiration and healing salve of hope."

Erin MacPherson, author of more than ten books, including the Hot Mama series

"Mary writes not as a spectator of life but as one who has lived it in all its broken beauty. The wisdom and grace she shares are powerful. I am grateful to call her friend."

Sheila Walsh, author, speaker, Bible teacher

"Mary DeMuth leads us into the presence of God through transparent lyricism. She reaches out a hand from a place of the broken and put back together, the fragile made strong, the poor made rich and draws us into a home for all who are hungry for Christ. This book is an embrace for anyone who longs to be known."

Emily T. Wierenga, founder of The Lulu Tree; author of *Atlas Girl* and *Making It Home*

"I desperately needed the message of this book: that my worth has nothing to do with my long to-do list and everything to do with God the Father's love list. This luminous, rich book taught me that we have worth in our sleep, in our failures, in our worst moments. Thank you, Mary, for showing me the faulty construction on which I was building my house. Talk about a fixer-upper! I'm excited to be 'reflooring' now and allowing the God who loves me to lay down a gleaming new foundation of worth and value."

Lorilee Craker, author of *Anne of Green Gables, My Daughter, and Me*; *Money Secrets of the Amish*; *Through the Storm* with Lynne Spears; and *My Journey to Heaven* with Marv Besteman

"With the voice of a trusted friend, Mary DeMuth invites the reader on a journey toward wholeness and worth. Each chapter is filled with authentic stories and practical help as Mary guides with deep empathy. *She's been there, she knows*, I kept thinking while I read this lovely book. And as one who knows, Mary takes you by the hand and leads the way to living loved."

Rachel Anne Ridge, artist and author of *Flash*

"On some level, each of us struggles with questions of worth. From the paychecks we cash to our personal appearance to the worries we lug alone in the dark, soul-pricking doubts curl up and take residence in our hearts. Are we enough? With sincere and bold truth-telling, Mary DeMuth debunks ten lies whispered by the enemy of our souls. *Worth Living* grants new perspective to see your life through God's eyes. You are wildly loved and made for a magnificent purpose. Equipped with the practical strategies and soul-searching questions of this work, discover God's grace anew and in joyful confidence leave those questions of worth forever in your past!"

Cherie Lowe, author of *Slaying the Debt Dragon*

"With clear, biblical insight and honesty, Mary grabbed ahold of my hand and encouraged my spirit with the truth—that I am worthy because of Jesus. You, reader, are worthy. Let Mary mentor you in these pages. Her stories, coupled with God's truth about who he created you to be, serve as a powerful weapon against the lies we believe about our identity."

Kris Camealy, author of *Holey, Wholly, Holy*;
founder and owner of GraceTable.org

"Mary DeMuth's gripping narrative of her journey through a childhood of abuse and abandonment to her desperate search for a father who would never leave echoes the heart's cry of a generation. In powerful prose, she exposes the deceptive devices of the enemy of our souls and solidifies the immutable message of a God who will never leave us, who will never forsake us, and who loves us beyond circumstance and crisis. For anyone who wrestles the monster of 'not good enough,' 'not smart enough,' 'not successful enough,' or simply 'not enough,' Mary's evocative authenticity will realign our vision of ourselves as God's adored 'enough' children."

Julie Lyles Carr, pastor, speaker, and author of *Raising an Original*

"*Worth Living* is a warm, steady hand at your elbow that leads you to the door marked 'I am beautifully made.' Mary's courage in revealing her own painful childhood and the steps she took to healing will help you open that door, walk into its light, and shine."

Margaret Terry, author of *Dear Deb*

"It's hard to find words vivid enough to do justice to the experience of reading Mary DeMuth's *Worth Living*. I found myself often nodding in agreement, occasionally smiling, several times brushing away tears. I saw myself in the struggles to find worth revealed in Mary's transparent telling of her own stories, and I felt less alone. But even more important, I found encouragement in the lessons she draws from the truths in Scripture that can combat the lies others tell us—or we tell ourselves—about who we are and what we're worth. This book is a treasure and a balm to be savored and absorbed."

Laura McClellan, writer

"Mary DeMuth is both a trusted BFF who gets me right where I'm at and a wise spiritual mentor who pushes me to grow beyond where I'm stuck. She empathizes with those of us who are crippled by criticism, who constantly push for production while craving connection, and who have an endless longing to belong. In *Worth Living*, Mary guides you on how to replace panic with peace, embrace your neediness as normal, and reunite with the woman you were created to be: a daughter of God's delight!"

Cheri Gregory, coauthor of *The Cure for the "Perfect" Life*

WORTH LIVING

how God's wild love for you
makes you worthy

MARY DeMUTH

BakerBooks
a division of Baker Publishing Group
Grand Rapids, Michigan

Published by Baker Books
a division of Baker Publishing Group
P.O. Box 6287, Grand Rapids, MI 49516-6287
www.bakerbooks.com

Printed in the United States of America

Library of Congress Cataloging-in-Publication Data is on file at the Library of Congress, Washington, DC.

ISBN 978-0-8010-0585-5

Unless otherwise indicated, Scripture quotations are from the *Holy Bible*, New Living Translation, copyright © 1996, 2004, 2007 by Tyndale House Foundation. Used by permission of Tyndale House Publishers, Inc., Carol Stream, Illinois 60188. All rights reserved.

Scripture quotations labeled AMP are from the Amplified® Bible, copyright © 2015 by The Lockman Foundation. Used by permission. (www.Lockman.org)

Scripture quotations labeled ESV are from The Holy Bible, English Standard Version® (ESV®), copyright © 2001 by Crossway, a publishing ministry of Good News Publishers. Used by permission. All rights reserved. ESV Text Edition: 2011

Scripture quotations labeled KJV are from the King James Version of the Bible.

Scripture quotations labeled Message are from THE MESSAGE. Copyright © by Eugene H. Peterson 1993, 1994, 1995, 1996, 2000, 2001, 2002. Used by permission of NavPress. All rights reserved. Represented by Tyndale House Publishers, Inc.

Scripture quotations labeled NASB are from the New American Standard Bible®, copyright © 1960, 1962, 1963, 1968, 1971, 1972, 1973, 1975, 1977, 1995 by The Lockman Foundation. Used by permission.

Scripture quotations labeled NET are from the NET Bible®, copyright © 1996–2006 by Biblical Studies Press, L.L.C. http://netbible.com. Used by permission. All rights reserved.

Scripture quotations labeled NIV are from the Holy Bible, New International Version®. NIV®. Copyright © 1973, 1978, 1984, 2011 by Biblica, Inc.™ Used by permission of Zondervan. All rights reserved worldwide. www.zondervan.com

Scripture quotations labeled Phillips are from The New Testament in Modern English, revised edition—J. B. Phillips, translator. © J. B. Phillips 1958, 1960, 1972. Used by permission of Macmillan Publishing Co., Inc.

Published in association with the literary agency of The Fedd Agency, Inc., Austin, Texas.

16 17 18 19 20 21 22   7 6 5 4 3 2 1

To my daughter Julia DeMuth,
who is stepping into her worth
with beautiful, brave assurance.

Contents

Acknowledgments

To my agent, Esther Fedorkevich, who cheerleads my worth on lengthy phone calls, thank you. I feel more worthy because of your words.

To Chad Allen and the fantastic Baker Publishing Group team for seeing a need for a book about worth and making it shine like a new penny, I appreciate all your labor on the book's behalf.

To my dear family, Patrick, Sophie, Aidan, and Julia, you've long shared that I am worthy. You've been the brunt of my own unworthy rants, and you've helped me lift my head toward joy. Thank you for loving me well.

To my prayer team, this book's success is the result of your many prayers during a difficult year in my writing career. We've been together more than ten years now, and look at what God has accomplished! Big hugs to Twilla (who now watches from heaven), Renee, Carla, Caroline, Cheramy, Jeanne, D'Ann, Dorian, Erin, Ginger, Helen, Holly, Jen, Kathy, Katy G., Katy R., Denise, Anita, Diane, Cyndi, Lesley, Leslie, Liz, Marcia, Marion, Marybeth, Pam, Paula, Phyllis, Becky, Sandi, Sarah, Tim, Tina, Tracy, John, Nicole, Tosca, Marilyn, TJ, Patrick, Jody, Susan, Ariel, Mary, Amy,

Acknowledgments

Lisa, Dena, Carol, Kathryn, Esther, Susie, Christy, Kimberly, Jodi, Ericka, Denise, Alice, Randy, Paul, Jan, Sophie, Sarah, Michele, Judy, Thomas, Heidi, Aldyth, Brandilyn, Phyllis, Teresa, and Sue.

Jesus, thank you for showing me my worth. Thank you for going to the cross to secure my salvation. Thank you for audacious love and the hope I have. You are worth giving my life for. Oh, how I love and adore you. This book is for your fame and glory. It's a testimony of the work you've done in my broken heart.

1

The Lie I Believed

You will be my own special treasure from among all the
peoples on earth; for all the earth belongs to me.

Exodus 19:5

I look down at my feet, long and lithe, as the Texas dirt grits
my toes and the sun warms them. I feel their connection to
the earth, grounding me, and I wonder, *Why am I here? Why do
I feel I need to justify taking up this one square foot of earth—to
play the games the worth stealers herald?* If I stand any longer in
one place, fire ants will swarm, then eat my toes for lunch—an
appropriate metaphor for the relentless pain of this struggle. One
thousand stinging ants telling me things like:

Look perfect.
Juggle well.
Achieve dreams.

Never fail.

Please everyone.

Stand out.

Shrink back.

All these mandates I perform for an ever-shifting audience of perceived critics. It's utterly exhausting. It steals my wherewithal and leaves me with welts on my soul.

This preoccupation with my worth started young, when teenage boys shoved five-year-old me to the ground, then stole my wide-eyed naivety under massive evergreens. My purpose then? To be stolen from. To be violated. And when I desperately needed to be rescued, no hero stood tall between me and those perpetrators. No parent drove a stake in the ground and said, "No more." Child Protective Services didn't intervene. No teacher discerned my pain. Very few adults took much notice of me as I wandered my neighborhood, skinned-kneed and waifish, searching for a friend in strangers' houses.

I learned this truth young: no hero existed other than me. And if I were to persevere to adulthood, the only person to deem me worthy would have to be me. I would take up my cause, run like the wind, and live scared and scarred.

And that's what I did. But not very well. Because how do you live when the refrain of *you're worthless* reverberates through you? When you know down deep you're a mistake?

I lived all those years of my childhood believing I was unworthy of protection, unworthy of affection, unworthy of attention, unworthy of applause, unworthy of nice things. I did not know Jesus yet. I was the biblical character Mephibosheth during King David's era, living exiled and assured that my limp disqualified me even from dignity, unaware that I had royal lineage pulsing through my arteries. Like my world, Mephibosheth's world imploded when

12

he was five years old. When news reached the palace that his father, Jonathan, and grandfather Saul had died in battle on Mount Gilboa, his nurse tried to smuggle him free, only to fall on the boy and cripple both legs—an injury he lived with the rest of his days. Without help, he couldn't escape; instead, he had to be carried from the foothills of Gilead to Lo-Debar, a town whose sad name means *pastureless*, to be raised by a stranger. The circumstances of life and the misstep of another eroded Mephibosheth's abilities and worth as he lived exiled on a scrub plain.

I relate. Do you?

Limping, limping, limping. There were days when my sadness and sense of worthlessness threatened my will to live. I wanted to die. Felt I deserved to rid this earth of me. There were days when I, as a young teenager, feeling parched and pastureless, did not see my mother or stepfather for hours and hours. My mom was busy pursuing another relationship, while my stepfather was toiling on swing shift. They often slipped into the house after I'd gone to sleep, and I lived life as an involuntary loner.

This was my state when Jesus found me. Lame of soul. Destitute of heart. Drained of strength. Outcast and needy. Desperately lonely.

Like King David who searched the kingdom for Saul's lineage to bless, God relentlessly sought me—and he relentlessly seeks you too.

At first I felt his advances must've been meant for someone else. (Have you ever felt that way?)

He spoke my name. *Mary.* My name means bitter and rebellion. But it also means wished-for child. And in an odd twist, I embodied the first two and longed for the latter.

"Yes, God?" My body shook. Was it from the chill of the northwest air? Sheer terror? Anticipation?

"Don't be afraid."

"All I've been is afraid."

"You are my child. I'll take care of you. I'll be the daddy you've needed."

"But I've had three fathers now, all of whom were nabbed by divorce and death. Are you sure you won't leave me?"

"Yes."

Fifteen years old at a weekend Young Life camp, I sat shivering beneath a behemoth evergreen, tears wetting my face, hoping against hope that God was truly real, that he had taken notice of me, the foolish and broken one. Scripture says God chooses the weak to shame the strong (1 Cor. 1:27). I believe that with all my heart. He can openly display his strength through those who limp. He's that kind of hero for me—and for you.

I wish I could tell you that the moment Jesus graced me with his strength I lived feeling worthy, my head held high, joyfully tackling life's mountains with vigor, no limp impeding my way. Instead, I still struggled. For years. And, honestly, I wrestle with feeling worthy even now. The question of worth still niggles me.

However, I feel more worthy than I've felt in years. More alive. More settled in my calling. Because I dare to believe that God, who starts works of worth, completes them in us (Phil. 1:6). Because I know it's possible to believe the truth about ourselves even when we've been bitten by lies for years. Because God is about redemption, and he sacrificially gave Jesus to buy us back to life. Because you are worth loving, and his love makes life *worth living*.

When King David encountered the son of his best friend, Jonathan, for the first time, he said the man's name. *Mephibosheth*. It means to banish or drive away shame. What an unusual name for a lame man who no doubt bore shame's heavy weight.

"Yes, sir?" Mephibosheth said, trembling.

"Don't be frightened," said David. "I'd like to do something special for you in memory of your father, Jonathan. To begin with, I'm returning to you all the properties of your grandfather Saul. Furthermore, from now on you'll take all your meals at my table."

Shuffling and stammering, not looking him in the eye, Mephibosheth said, "Who am I that you pay attention to a stray dog like me?" (2 Sam. 9:6–8 Message).

Mephibosheth voiced his utter worthlessness by comparing himself to a lowly dog, an animal much maligned by his people. And not only that, a stray—an unwanted nuisance, destined to die.

But eventually he must have shed a bit of that stray-dog shame. Because Scripture says this: "Mephibosheth lived in Jerusalem, taking all his meals at the king's table. He was lame in both feet" (2 Sam. 9:13 Message).

You may feel lame in soul and heart, but the truth is that you are loved by the Creator of the universe. He searches you out. He calls you by name. He tells you not to give in to fear, shrinking back from life. He invites you to "his banquet hall, and his banner over me [and you] is love" (Song of Sol. 2:4 NASB). Why? Because God loves who he creates. Dorothy Sayers wrote, "A work of creation is a work of love."[1] You are that work of love.

Are you weary of proving your worth? Worn out from running on the endless treadmill of expectations? Do you feel exiled from others? Like you're the only one who suffers from insecurity and angry, accusing voices?

You are not alone.

In addition to crippling circumstances and hurtful people, your worth, like everyone else's, is relentlessly attacked by the Father of Lies. He has made the lie a first-person declaration.

I am worthless.

I wonder if lame Mephibosheth coddled this deception in a land that valued the strength of a man. In our culture, which demands that a person have perfection, beauty, wealth, and fame to be deemed worthy, it's no mystery why so many of us battle feelings of worthlessness. Why you may fight these feelings.

So how can you spit in the face of the Father of Lies, who hisses such terrible words? How can you settle who you are (and whose you are) while standing on the rock of God's never-shifting love? How can you truly understand the depth of this love when you struggle to see that he even likes you? How can you take an honored place at his table, as a beloved child, when you lack the strength to even limp there? How can you believe in your sweet beauty when culture upholds impossible standards of airbrushed perfection? How can you live gloriously free, even if you don't measure up to one thousand ideals?

By believing the truth:

You are wildly loved.

You are more than a to-do list.

You are uncaged.

You are weakly strong.

You are secure.

You are beautiful.

You are chosen.

You are destined for impact.

You are worth more than a paycheck.

You are a redemptive story.

The life worth living can be yours if you dethrone the soul-killing lie that tells you you're not worthy and replace it with these ten audacious truths. Jesus said, "You are truly my disciples if you remain faithful to my teachings. And you will know the truth, and the truth will set you free" (John 8:31–32). My prayer for you echoes this: I long to see you set free from the tyranny of worthlessness, a shame I have carried so many years, because "you will be called, 'Sought Out, a city not forsaken'" (Isa. 62:12 NASB).

Although I've looked at my feet all these years and wondered why God created me to stand on this earth, I'm beginning to understand. Maybe I stand here to be loved. Maybe you stand here to be loved. Maybe the point is to sit at the feet of Jesus and rest there, not striving, not pushing, not jumping up and down, not rebelling to be noticed, not hollering. Just sitting at his feet, practicing our worthiness before the One whose worth outshines the stars.

2

I Am Wildly Loved

I am now utterly convinced that on judgment day, the Lord Jesus is going to ask each of us one question, and only one question: Did you believe that I loved you, that I desired you, that I waited for you day after day, that I longed to hear the sound of your voice?

Brennan Manning

LIE:
I Do Not Deserve Love.

The car ride to this place runs long and sweaty, while 70s music blasts songs about dead skunks or being high on cocaine. Two rivers run through—the Little Klickitat snaking east and west like an embrace and the Bloodgood, which crosses it. I know none of this geography, none of these water sources, because all this five-year-old can see is wheat, miles and miles and miles of golden stalks arcing as if praying. And suddenly, on the outskirts of Goldendale, Washington, I am lonely.

There are jobs there, for my mom, for her husband, my stepfather, Zach. We pull up to the small house—does it lean? The lawn is as overgrown as the wheat fields that front it.

The back shed becomes my special place to explore, a workshop decked out with glass and metal and wood—baby food jars suspended from boards, their lids screwed in. And inside each jar, a heyday of rusty mess. Screws. Nails. Washers. The shed reeks of rotting grass, but I endure it, naming it a quaint home in want of adventure. I make serpentine pathways through the tall grass, play Grateful Dead on the record player, and storytell my way to other worlds alongside an imaginary best friend.

I have relatively little memory of our time there other than pale loneliness. I cannot recall if we stayed four days or three months. I may have been a wild child left lonesome among the grasses with no playmates, but I felt nothing of the wild love of God in that blistering place.

I've heard it whispered that a child's understanding of love begins in the embrace of their mother, father, sister, brother. That our view of the Almighty tends toward those first vital relationships. Which all makes sense to me now forty-two years later. Because it's the loneliness that crushes me, the solitary figure of a blond-headed girl talking kindly to herself among the grasses, no parents in sight. Home did little to inform my worth. It certainly didn't give me wings, helping me soar in the knowing that I was loved, cherished.

I don't write this to impugn parents. I have made and am making my peace with my own (do we ever finally reconcile pain this side of eternity?). But today, I must go back to the place, the home-in-the-middle-of-the-wheat-field memory that typifies why I've felt so unloved all these years. I have not felt this way because of a slap across the face or angry words flung my way.

No. It was more lackadaisical than that.

It was indifference.

Apathy.

I grew up knowing my inconvenience. I understood that simply because I lived I was someone to tolerate. Certainly not cherish.

So I learned the art of shrinking. Of diminishing. Of being so obedient and quiet that the adults in my life never had to bother themselves with me. I played dolls. Didn't complain. Complied to a fault. Played hide-and-seek alone. I couldn't interrupt the partying, the working, the drags of sweet-smelling weed, the mundane tasks at hand to ask someone to read me a story. Better to stuff my childlike needs into the crevasses of my heart and stop demanding anything.

I will not ask for a story.

I will not ask for a favor.

I will not ask for a lunch.

I will not ask for an embrace.

Couple this need to be unnoticed (though, really, I screamed for notice) with what neighborhood boys did to me once we returned to Alki Beach, and I became warped.

Love? It meant making myself small so as to not be a bother. Or it meant giving my slender body to sex-hungry teens who told me rape meant love. But mostly love meant fending for myself, making a decision that not one human on earth gave a rip about me and that if I had to survive this lonely earth, I'd better pull myself up by my bootstraps and make it happen.

I became what the apathetic demanded—undemanding. I became what those boys treated me like—an object. But I knew very little of what it meant to live as the beloved of someone else.

I pinned all the tails on love's donkey in one place—at the feet of my father. My parents' divorce was finalized before I understood the complexities of marriage, perhaps even before I toddled. Every other Sunday, Jim (I never called him dad) rescued me from the indifferent parents and the raping boys and gave me what my soul craved—attention. I shined under the gaze of his blue-blue eyes. A dried-out sponge curled in the heat, I soaked up the water of Jim's attention that doused me temporarily back to life. But twenty-four hours every other weekend could not quench my thirst for love. And by the time I saw my father again, I'd be shriveled again, in want of water.

When my father left this world when I was ten years old, I stood before a coffin, shiny under the lights of a stain-glassed church, and curled into myself. When heroes die, you tend to do things like that, letting depression take you to the darkest places where you cry yourself to sleep, muffling the weeping with a tear-soaked pillow. Another decade later, I broke under the weight of truth—that my father, though he did love me, had a crooked side. He was a sexually addicted man who viewed women as objects.

So what is love? And how could I possibly be its recipient if love meant objectification?

Home taught me that love meant indifference or exploitation—two radical poles that had no happy medium. And in the bedrock of both apathy and a sexually charged environment, I decided I needed pedestrian love and that the only way to find it was to become the perfect little girl who did everything right, hoping upon hope that other people would find me worthy of attention.

So I begged for friends, searching the neighborhood, knocking on doors as a five-year-old, seeking someone who would bear the weight of my loneliness. And then I did my very best to become the kind of friend that fickle girls wouldn't leave. Loyal. Sometimes a pushover. Available. Willing to play whatever they wanted just so I would have a companion to fill the empty places in my life.

The performance extended beyond friendships. It seeped into that part of me that craved adult attention. So I studied and tried extra hard to catch a teacher's affirming gaze or, better yet, a big fat red A at the top of my paper. Throughout elementary school, I tiptoed this careful tightrope—living unnoticed at home, seldom demanding attention, becoming the best friend ever, even if it meant I donned the costume "pushover," outperforming my friends in math and science and reading and, well, everything so the adults would throw a scrap of praise my way.

This worked as long as I dared not break down at home. Or a friend didn't shapeshift, as elementary schoolgirls are wont to do in their fussy affections. Or a misstep in studying didn't land a B on my paper instead of that coveted A. As long as I could stay on the treadmill of perfect performance, I could live with myself, feel somewhat loved, and move throughout my life without asking deeper questions.

But at night in the quiet of my attic room, those questions demanded attention. Why was I here on this earth? Why didn't my family seem to want me? Why did I have such a cavernous hole smack dab in the center of my soul? Was I unlovable? What would finally make me feel like I was a girl who was wanted?

When I spent too much time on those pillow questions, the earth seemed to swallow my will, and depression stalked (though I could not have called it such a thing then). So I became stiff-necked, rededicated myself to proving my worth, and continued racing my way through life as a ten-, eleven-, twelve-year-old.

But with thirteen roared an unforeseen tremor that shook those questions from the recesses of me, right out into the blinking sunlight. I had once again focused my longing on one person, shifting it from my original father to my second stepfather, John. It seems the human heart craves that one person who can fill all, and mine was no different—though I did not know Jesus was supposed to be the one doing the filling. John loved me, listened to me, heard my worries, spent time with me.

But he would leave with the earthquake of divorce.

I despaired, while questions of my worth hollered and cackled inside my head. I wrote a suicide poem that involved a knife. But the blade terrified me, because I also fretted about hell, though I'd had no formal religious education to teach me of its flaming awfulness. Something told me I would die my way to eternal torment. That very real fear stayed the knife, but it could not answer the questions.

At fifteen, my wilted heart experienced a truly satisfying douse of water in the form of Jesus—the God-man who commanded seas, proffered feasts, and healed withered hands. I heard about him through Young Life, and every single week when someone stood up to talk about Jesus, I thought my own heart would renegade my ribcage and fly skyward. This Jesus seemed to have the answers to my pillow questions, seemed to care about the likes of me. I kept going to those meetings about Jesus parched, and when I walked away, the slaked thirst reminded me that something was different about this Jesus. He filled me up with love, which then overflowed audaciously.

I gave him my whole heart—aorta, ventricles, potential bypasses, blood aplenty—and asked him to be my daddy, to fill that insatiable thirst. And he did.

Jesus loved me.

This I knew.

But life had a way of interrupting the reverie.

Traces of this performing-for-love girl exist today. God sometimes feels terribly aloof, his love simply a word, a foreign idea. Or he seems capricious, disconnected from my life. Or exploitive. Or his affection depends on my perfection, so he gets hot-angry when I sin and is justified in turning his back on me.

We all have baggage like mine. It may differ in proportion or type, but the truth is we struggle to understand God's wildly audacious love for us. Our past experience is a lot like the filters in our home furnaces we are supposed to replace every few months—full of dirt and dust and mold, so much so that clean air becomes impossible. Because my filter was so full of gunk and grime, I easily listened to the lies that sounded like truth. I fed on them, then digested each morsel.

You aren't worth love.

You aren't good enough to receive love.

You don't deserve attention or affection.

Everyone else but you can experience love.

There's a reason you can't feel love—it's your unlovableness.

Those lies were continuously perpetuated, and I imbibed them. For years. I based my feelings of unworthiness on circumstances, tragedies, and deprivation. This tinged my view of God and his love for me. I could say all the right Christian words, even tell others, "Oh yes, God loves you so much," but at night, when my thoughts pushed their way in, I would think, *He sure does love them. But he can't love me.*

This is what happens when we base our understanding of God's love on anything outside of him. If his love depends on circumstances, then we view love solely through that dust-bunnied filter. If his love depends on our goodness, then we can never be enough to merit his affections. So we must take an adventurous step toward the only way we can know, really know, God's love: Jesus.

He said, "I am the way, the truth, and the life,"[1] which also means he is the way to understand the Father's love for us. We must hand Jesus our filters and our failures. We must immerse ourselves in the stories of the New Testament, where we see Jesus really love people whose circumstances were dire or whose failures shouted loudly. How did he react when those people approached him?

He loved.

He dignified.

He listened.

He healed.

He beautified.

We are no different. No different from the woman who had five husbands. No different from the prostitute who poured scented love on his earth-dirtied feet. No different from Peter, who denied his deity while roosters crowed his betrayal. No different from the disciples who fought to sit on the throne only he could take. We tend to think of those people featured in the pages of the Bible as unique, special, and wholly different than we are.

But we are all cut from the same humanity cloth. Kissed by the divine but bent on destruction. Broken by life. Halted by our own sin. Abandoned by others as we turn our backs on friends. We are clay-footed, needy creatures in need of love that transcends both circumstances and choices.

Our hearts need remodeling in the area of love, and it's not just a surface transformation Jesus desires for us. He invites us to a stripping of the drywall, a removing of walls, a gut job for plumbing and electrical, and an entirely new floor plan. Dust. Ripping down. Tearing out. Making way for the new.

The apostle Paul hints at this kind of radical transformation when he writes, "This means that anyone who belongs to Christ has become a new person. The old life is gone; a new life has begun!" (2 Cor. 5:17). I believe this down to my marrow, but I fear we see this as a once-only verse. In the moment we take the hand of Christ on this adventure called faith, all the old falls away, and the new life stretches before us in heavenly vistas. Yes, this was true when Paul wrote it to the Corinthian believers. But it is also true today—for us. We battle unworthiness nearly every day, and in that struggle, we build walls of protection, ways of coping, patterns of thinking. These old walls must fall away for us to understand our worth in an entirely new light. That's the power and beauty of sanctification. It's the now and not yet of walking with Jesus. We are continually being set free, or at least we have the opportunity to taste that freedom every single day, without borders, without walls.

But so many of us settle into the old house where lies about our worth scream louder than the encouraging voice of Jesus. And we think this is the house we were meant to live in. It becomes comfortable because the words are familiar. I write this because I still struggle. I prefer the old house where my unworthiness flaunts itself. It's entirely too scary to let God remodel.

As I write this, I sit in my office. Wood floors greet my feet. They are part of a remodel we did earlier this year. I love them so much. No more stinky carpet, soiled by pets and children and spills. Just clean, clean, clean. We have to remember that Jesus has to refloor us, discarding the used, soiled, dust-infested carpet of our insecurities and laying down shiny, hard flooring. It becomes the rock on which we stand. Love is the wood floor. And once you've walked on it, you find it hard to remember how you ever tolerated the carpet. You can't even remember what it was like to live that way.

I honestly could not remember the carpet until I pulled out pictures of our house before our renovation. It's the same amnesia we develop after God radically transforms our hearts, making them better able to receive his love and the love of others. You won't believe how amazing the transformation will be, so much so that you won't even remember what life was like when you denied your worth.

Peter uses the following housing metaphor with architectural and spiritual precision. He speaks of Jesus being our foundation.

Let these words wash over you. Believe you are chosen, precious, alive, and worthy to receive his mercy.

> So as you come to him, a living stone rejected by men but chosen and precious in God's sight, you yourselves, as living stones, are built up as a spiritual house to be a holy priesthood and to offer spiritual sacrifices that are acceptable to God through Jesus Christ. For it says in scripture, "Look, I lay in Zion a stone, a chosen and precious cornerstone, and whoever believes in him will never be put to shame." So you who believe see his value, but for those who do not believe, the stone that the builders rejected has become the cornerstone, and a stumbling-stone and a rock to trip over. They stumble because they disobey the word, as they were destined to do. But you are a chosen race, a royal priesthood, a holy nation, a people of his own, so that you may proclaim the virtues of the one who called you out of darkness into his marvelous light. You once were not a people, but now you are God's people. You were shown no mercy, but now you have received mercy.
>
> 1 Peter 2:4–10

You have received mercy. This is the truth. And Jesus ushered in that mercy, that audacious love.

Let's look at Jesus's life. Have you considered that Jesus also battled feelings of worthlessness? That perhaps he had a hard time understanding God the Father's love for him? The author of Hebrews wrote something so compelling, I'm afraid we miss the truth of it: "This High Priest of ours understands our weaknesses, for he faced all of the same testings we do, yet he did not sin. So let us come boldly to the throne of our gracious God. There we will receive his mercy, and we will find grace to help us when we need it most" (Heb. 4:15–16). Jesus faced every issue we face today, including questioning our worth, our insecurity, our fear that we're unlovable. But he came through without sin, believing his worth.

We Need the Mind of Christ to Change Our View

Mark Buchanan wrote, "First you shift the imagination with which you perceive the world, and then you enact gestures with which you honor it."[2] And perhaps this is why it's so hard to change our thinking about worth—changing our imagination is not an easy process. It's difficult to simply think in a brand-new way, especially if we have thought patterns that have become ingrained over years and years and years. Or maybe we've spent time ruminating on how we compare to our siblings or how one or both parents favored them over us. We may be replaying recordings of things we heard in childhood that came from people who were supposed to love us.

You're not worth my time.
You're in the way.
You should be seen but not heard.
You need to earn your keep.
You're only as good as your grades.
Your job is to serve me.

Those messages pierced our worth, and if we have not dealt with them, we've likely perpetrated the same lies against ourselves. We may be in a safe place right now, but the voices that hurt us before now sound a lot like our own.

I'd like you to take a moment to grab a piece of paper. Fold it in half vertically. On one side, write the worth-killing messages others have said to you or implied by their treatment of you. On the other side, note the voices you hear in your head that also nullify your worth. Compare the two lists. Who is the tyrant? If you're anything like me, your own voice is even meaner than the voices of others. You've somehow believed that to be made worthy, you have to follow in the footsteps (or mouthpieces) of the people who denigrated you. Because if you can keep yourself in check, reprimand yourself harshly for being less than, and berate your inadequacies, then maybe you can grit your way to becoming worthy.

Only it doesn't happen that way. It never has.

What child flourishes in an atmosphere of constant criticism? Typically, these children either shrink away into submission or flat-out rebel. Why do you think you will suddenly be any different when your voice accuses you? When has accusation ushered in long-term growth? Even God doesn't create growth and change in us through harsh measures. Paul affirms this: "Don't you see how wonderfully kind, tolerant, and patient God is with you? Does this mean nothing to you? Can't you see that his kindness is intended to turn you from your sin?" (Rom. 2:4).

Kindness leads to growth.

What does it look like to believe our worth? To believe God loves us? To live in light of that amazing love? We have told ourselves the wrong story all these years, that we are not worth love, that we have some sort of terrible flaw that alienates God from us, that we deserve poor treatment, or that in order to be okay, we must pummel ourselves with negative words, thinking this will somehow make us more worthy.

We are kinder to strangers than we are to ourselves. We shame ourselves and heap grace on others. And our heads have become havens for shaming, brawling, yelling, berating, humiliating. This is also exactly like the devil's voice. He steals, kills, and destroys *with his words* (see John 10:10). He is known as the accuser. "Then I heard a loud voice shouting across the heavens, 'It has come at last—salvation and power and the Kingdom of our God, and the authority of his Christ. For the accuser of our brothers and sisters has been thrown down to earth—the one who accuses them before our God day and night'" (Rev. 12:10).

When we stay in a constant internal accusatory state, we make Satan smile. Why? Because he knows if he can entice us to believe the lie of unworthiness, he can render us helpless and mute in terms of expanding God's beautiful kingdom. Put more pointedly: our belief in our smallness makes a small life. We keep our eyes on ourselves, our shortcomings, our pile of sin. We take our gaze away from God's ability to change us, the amazing power of the cross to redeem us, the truth of our worth in God's eyes.

Changing our minds about our worth is spiritual warfare, plain and simple. Choosing to believe the truth about God's love for us not only transforms us but also ripples outward into the lives we touch. We no longer do things out of worry or fear or guilt; instead, we live an abundant life based on our worth. We become irresistible to others who are hungry for our settled sense of worth and worthiness.

Our minds are transformed in many ways, the primary way being through Scripture. I encourage you to type out this long passage and place it somewhere prominent. Meditate on it. Consider it. Believe it. Trust that God purposefully orchestrated this Scripture passage with you (and me) in mind. Oh, how he loves you and longs for you to have his mind about you!

> "No eye has seen, no ear has heard, and no mind has imagined what God has prepared for those who love him." But it was to us that God revealed these things by his Spirit. For his Spirit searches out everything and shows us God's deep secrets. No one can know a person's thoughts except that person's own spirit, and no one can know God's thoughts except God's own Spirit. And we have received God's Spirit (not the world's spirit), so we can know the wonderful things God has freely given us.
>
> When we tell you these things, we do not use words that come from human wisdom. Instead, we speak words given to us by the Spirit, using the Spirit's words to explain spiritual truths. But people who aren't spiritual can't receive these truths from God's Spirit. It all sounds foolish to them and they can't understand it, for only those who are spiritual can understand what the Spirit means.

Those who are spiritual can evaluate all things, but they themselves cannot be evaluated by others. For, "Who can know the LORD's thoughts? Who knows enough to teach him?" But we understand these things, for we have the mind of Christ.

1 Corinthians 2:9–16

This shows that we have not received those words from Satan (the world's spirit) about our worth, but that God has freely given us his Spirit. And his Spirit will teach us to think the way Jesus thinks, to have his mind about ourselves. What is on his mind? His great affection for us. What is often on my mind? My shortcomings.

God sees our potential. We see our failure.

God sees us fully restored. We see our broken lives.

God sees our entire story. We see only our painful scenes.

God sees the future. We see the past and the present and despair about the future.

God sees his well-loved child. We see a Father who must be disappointed in us.

God sees his faithfulness toward us. We see our faithlessness toward him.

God sees our capacity to fail yet forgives us. We see our capacity to sin and holler at ourselves.

God sees how grace changes us. We see how gracelessness fails to motivate us.

God sees our return after we run away and embraces us as his child. We see our prodigal ways as proof of our unworthiness before him.

God sees Jesus when he looks on us. We see the worst part of ourselves when we introspect.

It's time we change the way we view things—by affording ourselves the same kind of grace we grant others but deny ourselves. The truth? We are not God. His ways are higher and kinder than ours. Remember, it's his kindness that woos us, not his harshness. We limit God by saying we are unworthy. We essentially insult our Maker by insulting his creation: us.

God created you.

He created me.

And we insult him when we question his handiwork.

In the book of Isaiah, God shared with the prophet why he selected certain people to perform certain roles in his plan. He said:

> What sorrow awaits those who argue with their Creator.
> Does a clay pot argue with its maker?
> Does the clay dispute with the one who shapes it, saying,
>   "Stop, you're doing it wrong!"
> Does the pot exclaim, "How clumsy can you be?"
> How terrible it would be if a newborn baby said to its fa-
>   ther, "Why was I born?"
> or if it said to its mother,
> "Why did you make me this way?"
>
> This is what the LORD says—
> the Holy One of Israel and your Creator:
> "Do you question what I do for my children?
> Do you give me orders about the work of my hands?
> I am the one who made the earth and created people to
>   live on it.
> With my hands I stretched out the heavens.
> All the stars are at my command."
>
> Isaiah 45:9–12

We are well-loved lumps of clay in the hands of the Potter. We are his amazing creation. And because we are image-bearers of the Almighty, we are mightily loved by him. The battle becomes fighting to believe that.

We Need to Reevaluate Our Relationships

The voices of others are powerful, and when people speak words of unworthiness to us, it's hard to believe otherwise. Some of these speakers have been family; others have been friends. In light of that, I've learned the importance of taking time each year to evaluate my relationships. Len Sweet wrote in a tweet, "Friend comes from the same root word as 'freedom.' A friendship that isn't 'freeing' isn't true friendship."[3] Perhaps you've had a relationship in which, whenever you're around that person, you feel the sting of judgment or fret over making mistakes, conjuring their ire. Instead of a relationship marked by freedom, it is a relationship in which you tend to cower or worry or shrink back. You don't allow yourself to be wholly you because you've learned that you are not enough for this person. As your relationship progresses, you change your behavior so you'll become exactly what the other person wants. However, keeping up a façade is debilitating and stressful.

Some of us project that same kind of fear onto God. We think he is like our legalistic friend or co-worker or family member who holds out a measuring stick and tsk-tsks us when we fall short. This dilemma has two solutions: (1) revolutionize our view of God or (2) consider modifying those damaging relationships.

In his groundbreaking book *Necessary Endings*, Dr. Henry Cloud talks about these kinds of people who eat at our worth, classifying them as fools. Fools are also highlighted throughout the book of Proverbs with nuggets such as these:

The fear of the LORD is the beginning of knowledge; fools despise wisdom and instruction. (Prov. 1:7 ESV)

A fool takes no pleasure in understanding, but only in expressing his opinion. (Prov. 18:2 ESV)

A fool's lips walk into a fight, and his mouth invites a beating. (Prov. 18:6 ESV)

Whoever trusts in his own mind is a fool, but he who walks in wisdom will be delivered. (Prov. 28:26 ESV)

A fool gives full vent to his spirit, but a wise man quietly holds it back. (Prov. 29:11 ESV)

If a wise man has an argument with a fool, the fool only rages and laughs, and there is no quiet. (Prov. 29:9 ESV)

Often when we push against a fool, they push back or minimize what they said, uttering something like, "Why are you so sensitive? I was only kidding." Cloud reiterates this when he writes, "The fool tries to adjust the truth so he does not have to adjust to it."[4] The problem with people who undermine our worth is that they don't hear our words but readjust them to their liking. Some people we love dearly suffer from narcissism. Others may simply be selfish. Some have become comfortable in being the hero in the relationship, which works as long as we remain the broken one to be fixed or controlled. While it's impossible to excuse yourself from every problematic relationship, it may be helpful to minimize your exposure to the people who consistently undermine you. This is not easy. It's not painless. And it will most likely hurt more as you set boundaries.[5] But take heart. The results in the long run (in standing up for yourself in a firm, kind way) will make this temporary pain worth it.

Cloud gives this advice in dealing with these kinds of people: "The strategy for foolish people is simple: quit talking about the problem and clearly communicate that because talking is not helping, you are going to take steps to protect what is important to you. Give limits that stop the collateral damage of their refusal to change, and where appropriate, give consequences that will cause them to feel the pain of their choice not to listen."[6] Again, this involves guts, love, and setting clear boundaries.

We Need to Remember How Much We Love Our Children

My husband and I sat across from a couple as they shared their recent grief. The man pushed away tears—I could tell he fought them—as he said, "I can't believe I'm worth God's love. I know what I've done."

"I'm writing a book about worth," I told him. "And believe me, the irony's not lost on me. I struggle in the same way."

"I remember the dark times," he said, "and I think, how could God find me worthy?"

"You just spent time telling me about how much you love your kids, is that right?"

He nodded.

"When I struggle with worth, I go back to how much I love my children. How even when they fail or make crazy choices or reject me, I still love them. Nothing they could do would change my love for them. I know you feel the same way about your kids, right?"

"That's right," he said.

"Now consider how much more God loves us. If we, being broken, can love our kids so fiercely, why do we doubt that God could love us even more?"

This all makes intellectual sense to us. We can reason it into existence, but we often reason it away by considering only our failings. We let fear rule our view of God's love for us. And yet, John tells us, "Such love has no fear, because perfect love expels all fear. If we are afraid, it is for fear of punishment, and this shows that we have not fully experienced his perfect love" (1 John 4:18).

Are you living in fear of punishment? Are you letting your own incomplete view of love, and perhaps even your own imperfect love, taint the way you perceive God's love for you? Or do you go farther back, remembering how a parent dismissed you, abused you, hurt you—and then project that parent's indifference and judgment onto God? I can't answer for you, but I can tell you I've done all these things. I've seen how judgmental I am of my own children and think God must be the same way. I've lived inside my head enough to remember the mean comments and judgmental condemnations directed at others that I never verbalized. I've assumed God's love for me always meant detachment or, because I felt in the way, that I was a grand inconvenience to him.

None of this is the truth. God's affection is greater than our small attempts at love. We cannot equate his love with our own failure to love like him. The kindness he shows us outshines our best selves on our kindest days. His love is loyal. In the Old Testament, the word *hesed* is used hundreds of times. It means God's loyal, covenantal love. It's based on his steady and faithful character, not our flighty ways. It's the kind of love that makes a married couple stay together through pain and loss and betrayal. It's the pursuing kind of love that welcomes home prodigals. It's higher, wider, deeper, and stronger than anything we can conjure up.

It's no surprise that we fail at understanding this outrageous love. It's entirely otherworldly. Completely alien. Our world runs on basic concepts of fairness and judgment, yes. But it also turns on the axis of narcissism and hyper self-adoration. When we stop for a moment and contemplate the crazy otherness of God's love, we become dangerous to our world system, don't we? If we dare to think of how much we love our children, then assign that love to God as a Father who loves his children even more, we are on the path of settling our worth. If our worth is settled, we no longer have to run around this life desperately trying to prove it.

We no longer have to use people's opinions to feel better about ourselves. We can give up trying to do so many things in order to garner applause.

The song "Jesus Loves Me" is desperately true: "Jesus loves me, this I know. For the Bible tells me so. Little ones [like you, like me] to him belong. They are weak [yes, weak], but he is strong [in love]." When we believe in his love for us, we are standing on holy ground, with nothing to prove. We no longer live in fear of condemnation or judgment. We freely and joyfully live as God's children. Just as children who know they are loved and protected are free to play to the edges of life, so we become free to dance, to fly, to bask in the smile of our Father while we play.

Paul summarizes this radically free life of living in the love of God. Please take a moment to let this Scripture passage permeate your heart. You've read it before, maybe one hundred times, yet I believe God wants you to see its truth in a new light. Read it once, slowly, thoughtfully.

> What shall we say about such wonderful things as these? If God is for us, who can ever be against us? Since he did not spare even his own Son but gave him up for us all, won't he also give us everything else? Who dares accuse us whom God has chosen for his own? No one—for God himself has given us right standing with himself. Who then will condemn us? No one—for Christ Jesus died for us and was raised to life for us, and he is sitting in the place of honor at God's right hand, pleading for us.
>
> Can anything ever separate us from Christ's love? Does it mean he no longer loves us if we have trouble or calamity, or are persecuted, or hungry, or destitute, or in danger, or threatened with death? (As the Scriptures say, "For your sake we are killed every day; we are being slaughtered like sheep.") No, despite all these things, overwhelming victory is ours through Christ, who loved us.
>
> And I am convinced that nothing can ever separate us from God's love. Neither death nor life, neither angels nor demons, neither our

fears for today nor our worries about tomorrow—not even the powers of hell can separate us from God's love. No power in the sky above or in the earth below—indeed, nothing in all creation will ever be able to separate us from the love of God that is revealed in Christ Jesus our Lord.

Romans 8:31–39

Now go back through the verses, only this time read them aloud.

Now grab a pen or pencil (or stylus) and circle the word *us*. Count them. There are more than ten.

Now draw a simple cross over anytime Jesus is mentioned and a triangle every time Paul references God.

Next, place a heart around every time love is mentioned.

Finally, put an X over any negations (no, not, nothing, neither).

Take a look at what you've done. It will look something like page 40.

One thing you'll notice is how much God and Jesus permeate this passage about love. You'll see how many times you (us) are mentioned. And you'll visualize afresh that nothing can separate you from his love—not even your own misguided perceptions of him. No matter how hard it is for you to grasp his love or how many difficult and painful things have happened to you, you are still loved. When evil assaults you, it cannot win against God's greater love, the kind of love that made him send his Son to die, rise again, and then spend eternity interceding on your behalf. It's unfathomable but true.

You may feel unworthy of such profound affection, but even that emotion does not taint the truth of God's love.

Your circumstances may rail against a loving God, but the truth is that his love never, ever fails. You may not understand it this side of heaven's shores, but it is true nonetheless.

God's love is bedrock. Build your life on it.

"What shall we say about such wonderful things as these? If God is for us, who can ever be against us? Since he did not spare even his own Son but gave him up for us all, won't he also give us everything else? Who dares accuse us whom God has chosen for his own? No one—for God himself has given us right standing with himself. Who then will condemn us? No one—for Christ Jesus died for us and was raised to life for us, and he is sitting in the place of honor at God's right hand, pleading for us. Can anything ever separate us from Christ's love? Does it mean he no longer loves us if we have trouble or calamity, or are persecuted, or hungry, or destitute, or in danger, or threatened with death? (As the Scriptures say, "For your sake we are killed every day; we are being slaughtered like sheep.") No, despite all these things, overwhelming victory is ours through Christ, who loved us. And I am convinced that nothing can ever separate us from God's love. Neither death nor life, neither angels nor demons, neither our fears for today nor our worries about tomorrow—not even the powers of hell can separate us from God's love. No power in the sky above or in the earth below—indeed, nothing in all creation will ever be able to separate us from the love of God that is revealed in Christ Jesus our Lord" (Rom. 8:31–39 NLT).

I want you to remember this. Believe it as if your life depended on it (and it does). God's great love for his Son is irrevocable, right? "And a voice from heaven said, 'This is my dearly loved Son, who brings me great joy'" (Matt. 3:17). Because of what that well-loved Son did on the cross, including experiencing the agonizing moment of being separated from his Father who loved him, we now are inaugurated into God's family. So how God loves Jesus is how he loves us. His perfect love for his perfect Son is now *ours*. You've no doubt heard it said before that when God looks on us, he sees Jesus because his death covers our sins.

If God's love for us is based on his love for Jesus Christ, *then we are safe*. We can live freely. Not to run around and gleefully embrace sin because of that freedom but to live fiercely loyal to the God who performed such an amazing act of love for us. He took our whippings, though he was innocent. He received our nails, though he was blameless. He faced our penalty, though he had no deceit in his mouth.

Galatians 3:26 says we are God's children through our faith in Jesus. Did you catch that truth? We are his children. And if we have a small understanding of how much we love and adore our children and multiply that by five billion, then we will still not understand or mine the love God has for us. (In fact, he loves our children more than we love them.) "So if you sinful people know how to give good gifts to your children, how much more will your heavenly Father give good gifts to those who ask him" (Matt. 7:11).

If you struggle to understand the love God has for you, then think of children climbing onto the lap of perfect, sinless Jesus. He didn't push them away. He didn't holler "unclean" when their dirtied knees touched his tunic. He didn't shun their exuberance. He welcomed them—just as you welcome your children home from school with an embrace and questions aplenty about their day. That kind of parental love is how God feels about you.

Rest there.

You couldn't have done a single thing to earn that love.

And there's nothing you can do that will unearn it.

Climb up onto his lap. Let him sing over you, calm your fears, set you free, cleanse you from the ick inside. He is the best Father a kid could ever have. And he loves you.

We Must Begin with Love

I recently read the book *Jesus Prom* by Jon Weece. The prose is simple but beautifully so. He writes these words: "John [the disciple] referred to himself as 'the disciple whom Jesus loved' (John 21:20). How do you refer to yourself? If you don't feel loved, it's not because you aren't loved."[7]

Weece's question is the question I have for you: How do you refer to yourself?

"I am the disciple whom Jesus loved." These are seven powerful words you must begin with every day. Modify it for yourself if you want and put it in present tense, but keep the sentiment exactly the same.

I am the girl whom Jesus loves.

I am the child whom Jesus loves.

I am the follower whom Jesus loves.

I am (your name here), whom Jesus loves.

This is how we must start, live, and end our days—on the bedrock truth of God's great affection for us.

· ·

TRUTH:

I Am Worth Loving.

· ·

Questions for Reflection or Discussion

1. When have you felt the most loved by God? The least? Why?

2. What could disqualify you from receiving God's love?

3. Who in your life is a terrific example of how to show God's love? How do they show it?

4. Which relationships undermine your worth right now? What is God saying to you about how to handle these relationships?

5. What insights did you discover after you marked up the Romans 8 text? What surprised you? Why?

6. If you are a parent, how does understanding your love for your kids help you grasp the depth of God's love for you?

7. What would it look like if you lived today in light of God's great affection for you? How would your day differ from yesterday?

——————————— WORTH PRAYER ———————————

Jesus, it's so hard for me to understand, grasp, or comprehend your deep, wide love. I filter that love through my circumstances, failures, and relationships to the point that I can't truly see you. Help me rediscover that you are for me, that you have great affection and love for me just as I am, whether I fail or succeed, cry or laugh, feel small or settled. I want to plant my life on the rock-solid truth of your love. This week, would you please show me specifically that you love me? Maybe through a special memory—a reminder that only you and I would know about. I choose right now to trust and rest in your love, absorbing it well so I can love the people in my life with wild affection. Amen.

3

I Am More than a To-Do List

I looked good on the outside, though. I was a dedicated student and high-achiever. I was a "good girl" who stayed away from big, obvious sins. But I couldn't relate to others without fear, and I couldn't trust God to love and save me on his merit, not mine. My life was all about earning and performing, and there was absolutely no place in that life for emotions.

Elizabeth Trotter

LIE:
I Am What I Produce.

I have built the tower of Babel. Only it doesn't resemble a ziggurat, a skyscraper, or even a mountain kissing the clouds. It looks an awful lot like a pile of to-do lists, one stacked on top of another, until the pile is so behemoth I cannot see past it.

I think we all struggle with the belief that our worth is tied to our production, and if or when that production wanes, our worth plummets faster than a bad stock. Perhaps an illness immobilizes us. Or anxiety prevents us from moving forward in our plans. Or maybe life has smacked us in the head with seven trials upon seven more trials, and we are unable to function as we used to. Some of this can liberate us from the lie that we are what we make, but many of us hunker down anyway and try harder, never believing that our mere existence merits Jesus's favor. But the truth is:

> We are worthy when we sleep.
>
> We are worthy when we're sick and cannot move.
>
> We are worthy when depression immobilizes our resolve.
>
> We are worthy when cancer steals our strength.
>
> We are worthy when age slows us way down.
>
> We are worthy when we fail.
>
> We are worthy when we fail others.
>
> We are worthy when our to-do list lies fallow, untouched.
>
> We are worthy when we hurt.
>
> We are worthy when we suffer persecution.

These are true statements, steeped in Scripture, baptized by the fact that we are image-bearers of our perfect Triune God. But so often we live as if these sentences are fairy tales, meant wonderfully for others but denied to us because we just can't get it together.

I felt my heart beat in my throat. To my left was a page, perfectly printed, which I was to replicate. Perfectly. As I tried I kept making mistakes—no space here, two commas instead of one there, transposed words, two capital letters.

I will do this. I will conquer this, I thought to myself.

Except that I couldn't, and tears eked from the corners of my eyes. Eleventh-grade typing class threatened to ruin my perfect grade point average, something I could not endure. If I got a B, I would be a failure.

So I typed. And mistyped. And used the correction tape.

Then I did what all brownnosing perfectionists do: I piled on the extra credit. I typed lines and lines about quick foxes. I practiced at home and brought the evidence back to school for a few more points. I stayed late to be tutored.

At one point, though, even all that work didn't make up for my poor skills. I cried in class. A friend leaned over to me and asked, "Are you okay, Mary?"

"No. I'm going to get a B in this class." I wiped away the tears, hoping my mascara wouldn't smear.

"Um, why is that a problem?" my friend wanted to know. "That is a good grade."

She was right, of course. My need for an A was irrational. But I couldn't tell her that. And I had to figure out a way to justify my tears. Crying over a B was just plain embarrassing. That's when the lie slipped from my mouth. "If I get a B, my mom will be so mad." This was a risk because my mom was a teacher at my high school.

"Really?" she said. "Your mom seems pretty calm about those things."

I mumbled something like "You don't understand" and kept mistyping.

I believe my keyboarding teacher took pity on me, noting all my hard, desperate work, and somehow I skimmed by with an A-. I exhaled when I saw it.

I would be okay.

Anything short of an A meant I had failed, meant I was no longer worthy, meant I had not lived up to my potential. Though

I sort of knew God loved me whether I flunked or aced a class, my actions told the real story of my beliefs: I was nothing if I was not perfect.

A few years later I sat hands poised above a different keyboard while my elderly piano professor walked me through a particularly hard piece. I desperately wanted to please this dear man with his age-wrinkled hands and quick, beautiful mind. When I sat on that bench next to him, I attended the school of life in the presence of his wisdom.

"I can't do it," I said, tears threatening.

"You think that if you cannot master something easily," he said, "it is not worth pursuing. But you are wrong. You can do this. Now try again."

I pecked at the piano keys. Made a mistake. Then another. He put his worn hands on mine. "This does not mean you're a failure, Mary."

I could not believe him. Didn't the definition of that word mean I had botched something? And didn't one small failure mean my entire being equaled failure?

I shook my head of his words. And I tried again. And again. And again. Until I played that piece perfectly. Except that perfectly wasn't enough.

"Your heart. It's not in it. You're playing mechanically. I want to know you are feeling the music," he told me.

"I can't." Those words were my go-to words when I didn't master something perfectly. I'd rather just give up than try again and risk repeat failure.

"You say that a lot. Take your hands off the piano," he said.
I obeyed.

With tears in his blue eyes and a smile on his ancient face, he told me he wasn't after perfection but heart. He wanted to know me, not applaud what I did. I was not my performance, he said. I was grateful for his words, desperately so, but I didn't internalize the truth.

I wish I could say I have drastically changed since those days. I may be less dramatic, but the old lies still hold me captive. Recently, my friend D'Ann talked about besetting sins, how it's typically one sin we struggle with our whole lives. It may take on different forms, but if we don't conquer it, we continue to circle back around to it. I nodded and immediately knew what mine was rooted in: working hard to prove my worth.

When I try like the dickens to do everything perfectly and on time, when I produce more than most people, when I rush danger-ously toward burnout, it is worth I'm circling back to. I'm like the toddler jumping up and down, wearing myself out at a party of adults where I perceive I'm unwanted. "Look at me! Look at what I can do! Notice me! See me!"

The problem is we seldom live our lives with the energy of a toddler.

Eventually, we grow weary of doing so much, and we either settle our worth or believe the lie that if we cannot produce as much as we used to, we deserve to feel unworthy.

We are starved for validation, seeking completed tasks as a rub-ber stamp of our existence. But as with the proverbial carrot at the end of a stick, a completed to-do list will never be attained. It's like the myth of finishing your laundry. Unless your entire family lives naked, and every scrap of clothing stands clean in neat piles, you will never finish that chore.

Before me on my desk is a list of my day's obligations inked in blue. Four things are crossed off (truth be told, they're the easiest tasks, not the hardest). Writing this chapter is one of them. And I fear I'll reach the end of the day without having completed my arbitrarily assigned work. Not completing my jobs will negatively affect my mood this evening. Sometimes I'll work late to make sure

I cross off everything. Every. Single. Line. And then I'll wake up the next morning dreading another list. The tyranny is not lost on me.

Why do we work so hard to ensure our sense of failure?

Why do we treadmill our way through life?

Why do we feel that sinking loss when we fail or drop the ball?

Why do we do things?

Of course there are simple answers. We have to make money to live. We feel God has given us things to do. We find a modicum of joy in our work. We have responsibilities to people, projects. We have to pay off debt.

But peel back the layers just a bit and ask yourself, "Why must I do all these things? What will happen if I don't? And how does that change my worth either way?"

Here are my painfully honest answers. I'm embarrassed to admit them so stark on the page:

I don't think God will love me if I stop.

God will be disappointed in me if I don't do all the things on my list.

But what I really mean is this:

I won't love me if I stop.

I will be disappointed in me if I don't do all the things on my list.

When we are enslaved to doing tasks, like I have been, we tend to worship the wrong god. And that god is an angry taskmaster who walks around this earth wearing our clothes and shoes and coats and gloves. That god is us. We have decided along the way that to be worthy, we must earn our way. We have failed to consult the Almighty on this meritocracy. We live our frenetic lives as if Jesus never came, never bore the weight of our shame and misdeeds and apathy on his sacred shoulders. We live as if everything is up to our stellar performance, not his ability to do amazing things through us. And when we fail ourselves, we project that disappointment onto God.

We cannot love others unless we first love ourselves, give grace to ourselves, allow ourselves to be human. And to love ourselves means we must be set free from being our own taskmaster, who is relentless and takes on many forms and taunts us with "if" statements that muddy our worth.

1. Perfection. (If I do things perfectly, then I will have worth.)
2. Rebellion. (If I rebel, I will test people's love for me, all the while wondering, *Will you love me even when I disobey?*)
3. Bullying. (If I demean others, then maybe I will feel worthy compared to them.)
4. Body image. (If I look awesome, then I will engender worth.)
5. Food. (If I can't feel worthy, then I can eat and find satisfaction in food.)
6. Relationships. (If I keep my relationships in perfect harmony, then I will have relational worth.)
7. Performance. (If I perform well, either onstage or by creating a façade and playing a role, then people will applaud my worth.)
8. Achievement. (If I climb this mountain, then I will finally settle my worth.)
9. Control. (If I can control the people and things in my life, then I will prove I am worthy.)
10. Money. (If I have money, then I will prove my worth in a tangible way.)
11. Sex. (If I experience sexual release, for that moment I will feel alive and worth pursuing.)
12. Escape. (If I escape the reality of my life, then I won't have to face my feelings of worthlessness.)

Reread those twelve "if" statements. Which ones resonate with you? Which ones don't? My "if" statements tend toward perfectionism, body image, achievement, and control with a huge dash of money lurking in there. Those twelve statements echo what the world screams to us about worth. We are worthy when we are strong, beautiful, in control, wealthy. We are unworthy when beauty fades, when friends walk away, when we get a "meh" reaction to our latest project.

So how do we get set free from the tyranny of all that trying and doing? How do we move from taskmaster Christianity to living in light of our worth?

Shut Out Those Shoulds

I live with a lot of shoulds. They are my companions most days. And the more I listen to them, the smaller and more defeated I feel. Some of mine include the following:

- I should write those thank-you notes.
- I should do that scary project at work—and now.
- I should call my parents more often.
- I should exercise five days a week.
- I should eat more veggies.
- I should volunteer more at school.

These shoulds are good. They add value. The problem comes when they become a slave driver and you can no longer discern between what God may have for you and what you feel you should do. Thankfully there's this important truth: your lack of doing doesn't nullify God's great faithfulness.

You truly, deeply need to rest there.

Because you know what? You'll always have the shoulds with you. The to-do list will be there in the morning. There is always more obligation than day. So with that realization, you can either say yes to everything or stop and learn to discern what is best for the day. And you can learn that stopping has its benefits.

Last week my eldest daughter called me. I was drowning in shoulds and, I'm sad to admit, saw her call as an obstacle between me and my list. As she shared her heart, I relaxed. I offered my perspective. Even so, when we hung up, I felt desperately sad.

Why? Because I am not sure I was quite *with* her in the conversation. My mind drifted to the things I needed to accomplish. Had I been more with her in the moment, I know I would have been able to give her what she truly needed—me.

Believe in God's No-Strings-Attached Generosity

As I gave my husband his regularly scheduled haircut, questions about my worth rattled inside my head. I was feeling guilty about the long-awaited remodel of our downstairs that was recently finished. In situations like this, my travels to third world countries really mess with my head. I thought of huts, muddy and dank, and then saw my farmhouse sink and thought, *Why should I have that?* So I brushed away the stray hair and looked at my husband, Patrick. "I have figured it out," I said.

He gave me that oh-no-what's-she-going-to-say-now look. "What is that?"

"I have given a lot of haircuts over the years. To you. To all the kids. And sometimes to myself."

"Yes, and your point is?"

"Well, it's just that if you add them all up at twenty bucks a pop—"

"Oh no," he said.

"What? It's just that if you add it all up, it equals what we spent on the downstairs. So in a way, I've earned it, right?"

He laughed at me. "Why can't something simply be a gift? Why do you have to earn everything?" he asked.

I rolled my eyes, more at myself than at him. Because he was right. It's an exhausting way to live to try to make the balance sheet of our lives work. If I labor this hard, then I get to have this. If I receive this gift, then I need to become worthy of it. If I do nothing, then I do not deserve anything. Yet God's grace trumps all this thinking. God gives us far more blessings than we deserve, and it's our privilege to receive those gifts, no matter how strongly we feel we don't deserve them.

Embrace Your Primary Job: Daughterhood

I sent an email to the Writing Prayer Circle, a group of people who faithfully pray me through every book I write and every speaking engagement I have, lamenting about my struggle with my work. My friend Liz emailed back. She wrote, "I finally got through all of my emails and read yours. I can so relate to every word of your snippet. I know so many others who also would be able to. I am struggling with worth still, even at my age. What worth does a PE teacher have when there are no PE jobs available, and no one will hire you for any other type of job because you don't have any relevant experience? I've heard that it's only men who struggle with their sense of worth and identity when they can't find a job, but it's not true (or I'm weird)."[1]

I assured her she was normal. We gain a lot of worth and identity from our occupations, and we experience very real frustration when our jobs don't meet our expectations or we lose a job. So many people see what they do for a living as the foundation of their lives. A person's job is one of the first things we ask about when we meet someone new. Our jobs define us and determine our place in the hierarchy of our culture.

But our jobs do not define our identities. Our status as God's loved daughters does.

I read a novel, *Lizzy and Jane*, about a woman who defines herself exclusively by her career as a chef. When life hands Lizzy lemons, and her dreams of advancing her career fall through, she says these important words: "I knew. I knew I could no longer justify my existence. No work could accomplish that. And if it couldn't, then it meant that I was more. I could be more, live more, give more—live large and thankful and with no regrets."[2]

We are more than our jobs.

We are more than our duties.

We are more than the next rung on the career ladder.

We are more than an advanced degree.

We are more than our paycheck.

We are simply this: women adored by Jesus. But getting to that place of knowing can be hard, especially if our drive for success blinds us to our need for rest, preventing us from slowing down long enough to reevaluate our lives.

Believe That Kingdom Math > Regular Math

I've seen this strange math at work in my career. No matter what I do, no matter how much I blog or market my books or how many radio interviews, ebooks, and webinars I do, it seems none of these contribute to that elusive goal of becoming a modest-selling author. I run on a treadmill of duties, never reaching the carrot of book sales dangled hopelessly before me.

So here I sit today, on the verge of tears, needing to know if it's okay to stop the marketing world a minute.

Have you ever been here?

Here's the kingdom equation I've learned: A + B *does not* = C.

Herculean effort doesn't mean success will come. And if you have that expectation of success (even in the slightest way), you begin to feel your effort means nothing in this world. And the flame of your wherewithal flickers in the wind, nearly extinguished.

I'm there. Feeling small. Tired. Needy. Worn thin. I am a girl standing in a snowstorm with a thin veil of clothing, unable to pull it tight enough around myself to make any difference. I'm a well run dry. A person with this vague sense that something or someone is beckoning me, but I'm too busy running to the next big thing to stop and listen to the whispers.

I love Jesus. But I'm scarily close to burning out for what I think is his sake. I teeter on the edge.

Once I spent time and money on a business coach who told me to embark on his surefire method of getting speaking gigs. Even though I felt in my gut that his formula had flaws, I chose to bend beneath my questions and follow the formula. I'm obedient that way. But that blind obedience cost me way too much.

And how many speaking gigs did I land by following his method? Zero.

And how many came through relational means? Several.

The Lord was clear with me after that frustrating lesson. "If you relied on a formula and found success, then the formula or your effort would get the glory. But if you let go and trust me, when I bring the increase, who gets the glory?"

We must be careful not to put all our eggs in the formula basket. We must be cautious about emulating gurus. We must become a bit cynical when someone comes along with a surefire method. Because, ultimately, God can do way more than what we expect. And if we limit him to our formulas, we hinder his work.

Remember That God Smiles When We Rest

We can become so absorbed in our jobs, roles, and lists that we shun resting. The more we work and try to prove ourselves, the less we're able to truly understand our worth as simply humans. As we push harder, we push God away, forsaking his refreshment in favor of frenetic activity. We fear that if we slow down, the world will crash. We'll blame ourselves for its demise and mourn the loss of our worth. If we don't do something, we can't be someone.

I love this piece from the beloved devotional *Streams in the Desert*. It speaks perfectly to our need for true rest.

> Straining and striving does not accomplish the work God gives us to do. Only God Himself, who always works without stress and strain and who never overworks, can do the work He assigns to His children. When we restfully trust Him to do it, the work will be completed and will be done well. And the way to let Him do His work through us is to so fully abide in Christ by faith that He fills us to overflowing. A man who learned this secret once said, "I came to Jesus and drank, and I believe I will never be thirsty again. My life's motto has become *Not overwork, but overflow*. And it has already made all the difference in my life." There is no straining effort in an overflowing life, and it is quietly irresistible. It is the normal life of omnipotent and ceaseless accomplishment into which Christ invites each of us to enter—today and always.[3]

Selah.

Pause.

Truth.

Since God rested on the seventh day, we can follow his example and pull away from our busy lives. We can retreat long enough to be rejuvenated. Rest is a holy act of faith through which we show we truly believe in God's ability to run the universe without our control or help. It's a pause that reminds us he is doing his work, and our ceasing from work reveals our level of trust in him.

But we believe the lie that what we do and how much we produce equal our worth, so we expend ourselves until we burn out, and we're left in worse shape than before. I've touched burnout. I near it way too often. There have been times I've actually longed to be sick enough to be in a hospital just so I could lie there, mindlessly watch TV, and retreat from the panic of an overworked life.

Let me ask you this: How does overworking glorify God? Doesn't that show that you've decided nearly everything in your life is up to you? If you must do all the things, and failure is not an option, where can God step in? Rest is the avenue where you let God be God and you be you.

As I've been processing my productivity and my proclivity to burnout, I've stumbled on a lie I've believed in the pit of my gut. Here it is: if a thing can be done, then it must be done.

This belief is tyranny. And I've lived under this dictatorship most of my life. Not only that, but it's getting worse. I simply cannot *not* do something. If my brain conceives something, I must do it. Or if I see a loose end, it must be tied up neatly—and always by me.

No wonder I'm tired from all this obsessive compulsion!

What would life look like if we left things undone, if we learned the artful joy of neglecting tasks?

Sickness teaches us this. We learn in times of nonproductivity that the world spins on its own without us do-do-doing everything. And we understand that what we do doesn't equal who we are. This is difficult for the achiever in me, which is why I often jump back into the rat race, thinking—wrongly—that the more I do, the more I'll finally feel worthy.

The treadmill keeps moving, and I find myself tripping more and more, bruised by my own relentless expectations.

The way out for me? For you?

Jesus.

Surrendering to him, to his Sabbath. To rest from labor so we realize the world doesn't depend on us. To trust God for his work within us rather than our busywork for him. To slow down enough to hear, "Well done, good and faithful servant." To stop equating our worth with production.

This weekend I will rest again. I will let my to-do list lie fallow. I will take a walk, marvel at the trees, sing a few worship songs—all to rid myself of the lie I have believed for so long: if a thing can be done, then it must be done.

Let Go of Productivity and Embrace Purpose Instead

Perhaps you battle indifference or exhaustion at your job. Or you work hard at something that does not bring satisfaction. One thing we all need to understand and internalize is purpose. I can scrub toilets joyfully if I know there is purpose behind the act. We need meaning to help us persevere in the obligations of life. Robert Quinn asserts,

> During our life we often experience periods when we seem to lose our sense of meaning and purpose. There is no longer a feeling of alignment between our inner values and our tasks in the external world. We find ourselves working harder and harder and receiving less satisfaction from our efforts. We struggle through every day, lacking the vitality, commitment, and initiative we used to have. After much inner reflection and contemplation, we begin to realize that we need a new focus, a new vision, but it is difficult to uncover.[4]

Have you lost your focus or vision? Has the "why" of your lists eluded you? If you're like me, you want to live this life well. You want to look back on what you have accomplished and feel that, to the best of your ability, you did what God handed you to do. What if you simply do ten thousand things but without purpose? Will those things matter? Only God can sort that out, but I do resonate with what Jim Loehr writes: "A flawed purpose always results in a flawed ending. . . . And because more than half our waking life is consumed by work, how we frame this story is critical to our chance for overall fulfillment and happiness."[5]

If you're faltering in your worth, and your work feels purposeless, take a moment (or several moments) to seek God.

Why are you here?

What makes you unique on this earth?

What is God's overall plan for his church? For his followers? For you specifically in your community, with your talents, with the relationships he has placed you in?

Delving deeper into purpose will help frame your worth. I had to write a branding statement for my work. After some false starts, I finally chose *re-story*, which perfectly captures where I am and who I am and why God placed my feet on this earth. My purpose is to help you find a new story too.

I'd like to challenge you to write a purpose statement. Don't make it generic. Resist making it sound like a Christian greeting card or something your pastor would approve. There is only one you in this world, and you have a unique purpose to fulfill. You may work with your hands to create art that stirs people's imaginations. You may revel in getting on your hands and knees to play with preschool children. You might prefer life out of the limelight, writing cards to people who are lonely. You could be called to do significant work in prayer, interceding for others in the shadows. Whatever it is, pray that God would reveal it to you, and embrace it. Don't dismiss what he shows you because it isn't what I do or that woman does or that leader does. We don't need another them. We need you.

If this exercise stumps you, send an email to ten people who know you well. Ask them, "When you think of me, what is the first thing you think of? If you could describe me in a few words, what would you say?" Compile all the responses in a document and start circling the similarities. Sometimes we're so stuck in our own head that we can't see ourselves clearly, but those who love us can. Rely on their wisdom to discover your purpose.

The word *re-story* came to me after reading several emails like the one I encouraged above. And even then, no one said, "Hey, you're the 're-story' lady." But one day God wrapped up all those phrases and sentences by whispering the tagline to me directly. What an amazing, sweet God! I believe he will do that for you too.

Let's pause a moment and pray for just that.

Jesus, I pray that you would gently and beautifully reveal my purpose. Help me embrace that purpose—not run from it, not judge it, not dismiss it. Thank you that you have a great plan to enact through me, that I will touch people whom no one else can. Thank you for placing me where I am. Show me what it means to serve you with gusto in my job, my daily life, and my family. Please reveal my sweet purpose soon. Amen.

Have Your To-Love List Overpower Your To-Do List

People are more important than action items. I'm praying to return to that truth and live my life better in light of it. I hope to become more interruptible, more fluid in my ability to set down perceived duties for the sake of people. I would like us all to be free from having to say yes to every opportunity so we can say yes to the truly important people God sends our way.

Our worth increases when we strive to dignify someone else's worth, when we stop what we are doing simply to be available to a friend, a spouse, a child, a relative, a friend. We participate in the kingdom of God when we realize people trump productivity.

We are more than what we do. Our worth is dependent on our daughterhood to an Almighty, merciful God. We do not have to jump up and down, hoping to garner his gaze. No. We are loved simply because we exist. I admire what author Tim Hansel says:

> We may desire to bring the Lord a perfect work. We would like to point when our work is done, to the beautiful, ripened grain, and bound up sheaves, and yet the Lord frustrates our plans, shatters our purposes, lets us see the wreck of all our hopes, breaks the beautiful structure we thought we were building and catches us up in His arms and whispers to us, "It's not your work I wanted, but you."[6]

TRUTH:
My Worth Flows from My Daughterhood to a Loving Father.

Questions for Reflection or Discussion

1. Look back over the "if" statements in this chapter. Which of these have you uttered to yourself? Would your best friend agree with your assessment?

2. When was the last time you "shoulded" all over yourself (did something solely because you thought you should)?

3. How does thinking about God's generosity change the way you view your own tasks for the day? What would it look like if you rested from your to-do list?

4. Who in your life best exemplifies the daughterhood of God? Why?

5. How does understanding the upside-down nature of God's kingdom help you view your daily work?

6. Is it difficult for you to rest? Why or why not?

7. Grab a piece of paper or find a journal. Write down who is on your "to-love" list. Take some time to pray today for each person on your list.

WORTH PRAYER

Jesus, thank you for completing the work on the cross. I cannot do anything to add to your extraordinary act. Yet I spin my wheels trying so very hard to please you. Help me slow down and rest. Settle me into your love so I know that I am worthy. Keep me full of peace, not striving, not overproducing, not bordering on burnout. I'm so tired. Would you please renew me? Thank you for making your yoke and your burden light and for wanting to give my soul rest. I choose today to quiet the taskmaster and, instead, listen for your sweet, quiet voice. Amen.

4

I Am Uncaged

Let the past sleep, but let it sleep on the bosom of Christ.
Leave the Irreparable Past in His hands,
and step out into the Irresistible Future with Him.

Oswald Chambers

LIE:
I Will Never Overcome the Past.

My mind often drifts back to the way-back-when times—those childhood memories that seem to snag at my worth. Some of them are monsters; others seem ridiculously benign.

The benign one: I am alone in a hoof-pocked pasture, trekking the back ten acres, humming to myself, wishing for a friend to share the walk with, settling for the one-sided company of myself. I jump the trench that leads to the woods surrounding a small creek

65

and then push my way through underbrush to find a clearing where the birds sing louder and the sun spotlights the earth.

I take off my shoes, tentatively pick my way through the burrs, and find cold, slippery rocks. The rush of pure water steals my breath, shocks me alive.

I stand there, feeling immensely small, watching the birds circle in the sky above. If only I could soar like them, I think. I slip my bluing feet into dirty socks, pull on my shoes, and trod my way back home, the place where I feel insignificant and unworthy, caged by my own lonely mood.

It's a pedestrian memory, but it embodies so many days I felt alone during my childhood.

And yet God is not simply the God of way back when but of Tuesday and of last January and of that fight you had two hours ago. As the great I Am, he lives within the beautiful present tense of us all, wholly available to us by the Spirit residing within us. I picture the Spirit sometimes as a bird with a key in its elegant beak, and that key opens the cages we've been in. Sometimes those cages are ones we've crafted with our own hands by choosing bitterness and unforgiveness as coping strategies. Sometimes others create those cages by angry words, caustic actions, or malicious intent. Regardless of how the cage came about, the Spirit has the key to unlock the iron door and set us free to fly.

The problem comes when we prefer the so-called comfort of a barred life to the open air of freedom. And whether ancient or fresh injuries placed us there, we have the choice to either stay inside the open-door cage or risk life in the great big world.

Honestly, the cage feels quite cushy.

Consider these verses: "The high priest and his officials, who were Sadducees, were filled with jealousy. They arrested the apostles and put them in the public jail. But an angel of the Lord came at night, opened the gates of the jail, and brought them out. Then he told them, 'Go to the Temple and give the people this message of life!'" (Acts 5:17–20). The apostles had been arrested and imprisoned, but God set them free. They went from being caged in a prison to soaring free and sharing the message of Jesus. God literally uncaged the apostles.

And yet, here I sit, unable to flee my confines. Maybe you feel incarcerated by the past, and you can't figure your way out. There are many prisons we find ourselves in, and the longer we stay inside, the more comfortable they become.

Some of these include:

The cage of a broken friendship. Maybe someone you know is filled with jealousy and, through selfish actions, has imprisoned you (spread rumors about you, yelled at you, put you in your place).

The cage of a painful childhood. Maybe you feel like your past is its own prison, with painful flashbacks. Maybe you feel like you're doomed to repeat the sins others committed against you and you're helpless to change.

The cage of unmet expectations. This comes from when you fail someone or someone fails you. You spend your life wallowing in the jail of wondering why, rehashing the incident, and believing (wrongly) that this one act has ruined your life forever.

The cage of strife. Maybe you're currently in the midst of a conflict so painful that you can't seem to ponder anything other than heartache. You cannot find joy because of the conflict. You spend time thinking of clever comebacks and ways to win the argument.

The cage of apathy. Life has been so difficult that you've given up completely. You simply have no energy to love others, take care of yourself, or do one more thing. You just don't care. And that not caring has placed you in a cage of doing nothing, feeling nothing. Lethargy is your happy place.

The cage of control. Some of us are in prison because we've tried to make something happen (or someone change), and we spend our entire lives trying to orchestrate outcomes. All we do is connive to make things happen without realizing the futility of our efforts.

The cage of bitterness. It's the darkest of dungeons, this jail cell of bitterness. It prohibits joy and makes us think vengeful thoughts. It harbors unforgiveness, causing us to build huge walls around our hearts so no one else can hurt us. When we do this, we also cut ourselves off from the life that brings joy and abundance. No pain. But also no love gained.

The question becomes: Do you long for freedom?

Do you want the shackles of shame, bitterness, control, and broken friendships to fall away?

Do you desire to breathe the air of the free, inviting skies?

Is the trajectory of your life moving toward prison or emancipation?

There is hope. And it's found in Jesus. To settle your worth before him, give him your regrets, hurts, anger, confusion. He sets captives free, gloriously free.

What would have happened to the apostles if, after the angel released them from prison, they remained there, lamenting their lot? We'd call them stupid. They had been freed! Yet, thankfully, they walked in their freedom. They spent their emancipated days loving others and telling them about Jesus. That's God's heart for you today—he wants to set you amazingly free so you can share this beautiful freedom with others.

You were not meant to live a caged life. Bars should not cover the windows of your heart. Recognize your freedom and live that way.

That's easy to say, but so often reality disrupts our pursuit of freedom.

This happened to me one day when an old friend popped into my mind, clear as a melody. She was a friend I'd known very well when I was a new mom. She lived in an unusual house with an unusual layout in an equally unusual location, but she didn't let that stop her from inviting people into her family's life. She was beautiful, loyal, and fiercely intelligent. Honestly, that's all I thought about when I started searching the internet for her name.

I didn't find much, but enough to scratch out an email address.

I emailed her. Told her how I was doing—the typical chatty, how-have-you-been-all-these years email. I waited to hear back. Wanted to know how she had fared over the decade. But her response was curt. Searing. Abrupt. A few simple sentences with no invitation to continue the conversation. I knew that would be our last communication.

This small exchange stewed inside me all day and bothered me throughout the week. Why had she been so short? Anger lived in the undertone of her words.

Then I remembered.

She'd been connected to another friend, one whom I had hurt. I won't try to convince you of my rightness; I tend to think we like to be the heroes of our stories. But as I've looked back over this painful situation in which I no doubt hurt a friend, I've been able to reimagine it from the friend's perspective and can see why the woman I emailed would be curt with me.

Still, sometimes the past will not let us go, particularly when regrets stain the memory. Sometimes there's absolutely nothing we can do to resolve a situation, fix someone's perception of our actions, or apologize our way into the heart of someone we've maligned. What do we do in that case? How do we not let our own foibles inform our worthlessness?

Believe me, I heard the voices loud and clear after I got that email and realized the reason for her tone. *This will never be repaired, and you deserve every ounce of disdain and ire. There are people who roam this earth who do not like you. You will have to live your days knowing this truth, and there's simply nothing you can do about those who see your picture and grimace. Because, really? Your worthlessness caused this problem. And you deserve to suffer for it. Only a worthless person hurts others.*

Have you experienced this? Ever believed that because you cannot repair a relationship, your worth nears zero? Or do you rehash an argument over and over again, thinking of what you could have said until it nearly makes you sick with fretting? Now that you are wiser, do you regret a period of time in your life and despise the person you were back then?

You are not alone. Humans hurt one another. It's a universal foundation we can build a skyscraper on. It's a double-edged sword. If someone has insulted us, demeaned us, or hurt us, then our worth is undermined. We believe the lies, particularly if the person is important to us or just extremely persuasive. If we have harmed someone else, then we have to combat the voice that says, *Only a monster would treat someone like that. Who are you? You are not worthy of affection or love. You are irredeemable, and this thing you did will color your life until you die.*

How do we battle against such pain? The answer lies in speaking, believing, and living the truth of the human condition. Not one human being on this green globe is sinless. None of us lives life perfectly. We are a tangle of past hurts and present regrets. We must find our worth outside our performance in our relationships. Specifically, we must find our worth in one relationship: with Jesus Christ.

Our past does not sum up our worth. Because we serve the God of the present tense, we can rest knowing that he loves us, regardless of what we've done or what's been done to us. He sees the entirety of our lives as a breathtaking story. Thankfully, even our disobedience or poor choices from the past cannot thwart his purposes on this earth today, tomorrow. He is big enough to redeem what seems insurmountable to us.

Grief Doesn't Indicate a Lack of Healing from the Past

I used to think that if I was sad, or I grieved, then something was terribly wrong with me and I hadn't fully healed. In those moments, I forgot all about Jesus in anguish in the Garden of Gethsemane or his weeping at the tomb of Lazarus or his crying out to God the Father in agony on the cross.

Jesus grieved.

And he grieves alongside us. Just because we mourn does not mean he hasn't begun the process of uncaging us. In fact, I would argue that grief is the threshold we must cross in order to be set free from the past. We must realistically mourn what wasn't right, how we weren't right, how suffering entered in.

My friend Sarah resonates with this truth. She writes:

Being healed from our hurts doesn't mean we don't still feel their pain. I had the belief that the two things were tied together: healed equaled no pain. And so when the pain would resurface, I felt like I had lost progress toward healing. But now I see how that thinking was wrong. I am healed from those hurts, but when I think on those moments, pain will always be felt. And that's okay. That's normal. Shutting it off does no good. Denying it only tells me that I am not worth the tears.[1]

This grief is not limited to the far past. When we focus on grief from decades ago, we tend to minimize last year's hurt and forget that we, too, need to be uncaged from the recent past.

For me, that recent past involves a foreign country, a dream lost, and fresh grief.

Wide-eyed and full of optimism, my family moved to France right after Patrick finished seminary. We were going to share Jesus with so many! Our children would thrive! We would learn the language! Life would be full of amazing food, great conversation, and sweet worship in French.

While many of those things happened, mostly I fell apart, dancing dangerously close to the type of depression that immobilizes or institutionalizes you. Our time there had been so extreme in terms of trials that counselors diagnosed both of us with post-traumatic stress disorder (PTSD). Even eight years post-France, our children still bear scars. I know I do.

The heartache associated with church planting there is still so great that I cannot return to the southern coast of France (at least not yet) without fear of falling apart. So much for optimism. The greatest pain, of course, was our children's suffering, something I'll regret and apologize for the rest of my life. The second greatest pain, however, was relational, and all that occurred within the structure of Christian leadership. I still cannot write the story, not specifically. Some things are not meant for print, I've decided. But suffice it to say, I carry the scars in my heart today. I'm more suspicious, certainly quite jaded and pessimistic. I don't accept people at face value anymore. I question motives. After all, if Christian leaders could act in such an unbecoming way, then aren't all of us suspect? And why in the world would I choose to trust anyone?

I'm confident in saying I'm uncaged from the way-back past, but I still push against the near past, and it haunts me now. So why am I sharing this with you? Because I value honesty. And I want you to know that even as I pen this book on worth, pain sometimes cages me, preventing me from flying toward joy.

And sometimes it seems the more recent pain crushes our worth more than the echoes of the past. Why? Perhaps because it's fresh. We remember it more readily. The tunnel of that pain is new, and we cannot see beyond the dark bend.

Difficulties Are Freedom Blessings in Disguise

"Many are the afflictions of the righteous, but the LORD delivers him out of them all" (Ps. 34:19 NASB). I love that verse. Why? Because it states reality so beautifully. It doesn't say, "Those who trust God never have heartache, because God sees to it that nothing bad ever happens to his saints." It says the truth. We who are righteous (by Jesus's sacrifice on the cross on our behalf) are afflicted in this world. But God delivers us.

Think about it this way. God is a loving parent. He wants his children to trust him. He sees when we're walking down difficult paths, but he also knows if he delivers us too soon, we might think (wrongly) that we delivered ourselves from the peril. So he waits. And we rail. And fight. And yell sometimes. Why has God left us afflicted? Doesn't he love us?

The deliverance he brings is always in his perfect timing. And I firmly believe it's sweeter the more we're afflicted.

Sometimes folks ask me how I am so close to Jesus. Honestly, there are days I feel really far from him. I stumble through this life like all of us do, living more caged than uncaged. But I've had to trust him through difficult times, and I've found him to be faithful time and time again.

"The LORD is near to the brokenhearted and saves those who are crushed in spirit" (Ps. 34:18 NASB). Maybe he seems so near to me because I walk a path of brokenheartedness. If you feel brokenhearted, remember this verse. Revel in your brokenness, because Jesus is near.

Your Past Need Not Be Your Present

Speaker Bianca Olthoff shared this familiar phrase at an event I once attended: "Hurt people hurt people." But then she said this: "Freed people free people." And oh how I resonated.

You may have hurt or damaged others. Others may have hurt or damaged you. But because of Jesus, hurting is not your fate. You don't have to resign yourself to messing up others or wallowing in the mess from the past. Yes, it's true. Hurt people hurt people. Damaged people damage people. Messed up people mess up people. But it's truer that Jesus overcomes all that hurt, damage, and mess.

After I heard her say, "Freed people free people," I wrote a few more truths in my journal. Let them sink in as you read:

Healed people heal people.

Reconciled people reconcile people.

Loved people love people.

Joyful people enjoy people.

Renewed people renew people.

Graced people grace people.

Hope-filled people instill hope in people.

Open people open people.

Mended people mend people.

Soothed people soothe people.

Rejuvenated people rejuvenate people.

Improved people improve people.

Restored people restore people.

Cheerful people cheer people.

Revived people revive people.

Delighted people delight people.

Go ahead, replace the words right now, the words that have defined your life in the past. *Damaged. Messy. Broken. Hurt. Deconstructed. Maligned. Hopeless. Unregenerate.* Replace them with some of the words above. *Renewed. Delighted. Healed. Restored. Rejuvenated. Revived.*

You cannot reach freedom today without acknowledging the slavery of the past. As God turns your damage to healing, an amazing transformation happens. You not only embody the positive trait but also emerge as an agent of healing for others. That is the power of being uncaged by Jesus. You are uncaged to be an uncager.

So be brave. Face the past. Mourn it. Grieve the pain. But don't stay handcuffed to it. Don't let your heart become complacent. Don't believe the lie that you are the sum of your pain—or the equally true lie that current pain proves your unworthiness. Jesus is no longer the sum of his pain on the cross, because there is more to the victory story. Death, yes. Pain, yes. Betrayal, yes. Grief, yes. But then? Uncaged resurrection.

· ·

TRUTH:

Jesus Helps Me Overcome the Past and Find Lasting Joy.

· ·

Questions for Reflection or Discussion

1. Take a moment to watch birds today. Write down five observations about them. How are you like them? How do you differ?

2. What cage do you find yourself in today (unmet expectations, strife, apathy, etc.).

3. How has grief prevented you from understanding true freedom?

4. What is your greatest grief today? How has God walked alongside you? Where have you felt abandoned?

5. What current difficulties cause you (perhaps) to lose faith in God's goodness?

6. What trials have made you grow the most in the past decade? How did God use those pains to set you free?

7. Look over the list that begins, "Healed people heal people." Which of those phrases best represents your desire right now? Restoration? Delight? In what ways has God used your past to uncage others?

WORTH PRAYER

Jesus, I desperately want to be a flying, unhindered bird, soaring above my problems and issues. Forgive me for preferring the cage to living free. Help me understand why I stay stuck. I desire to see grief and difficulties as means to run to you for help instead of blaming you for them. Restore me so I can be part of your restoration of others. Renew me so I can be an agent of renewal in this sin-sick world. Revive me so I can reveal the true life of you in me to those who long for reality, change, and deep abiding life. Amen.

5

I Am Weakly Strong

Long lay the world in sin and error pining
Till he appear'd and the soul felt its worth.

"O Holy Night"

LIE:

I Should Be Ashamed
of My Weakness.

I remember weeping. I was not the pretty teary-faced girl who sniffed in her sadness, then took a sublime sip of tea. No, this was a guttural cry that caused my diaphragm to ache hours later and my eyes to puff up and sting in the light of day. I sat in the yellow-walled living room of our tiny home in France, and I erupted. One of the members of my church-planting team looked at me, slack-jawed. If I'd attacked him with knives, he'd have looked less surprised.

The tears came from betrayal. Again. And they continued because the pain had that awful quality of continuing on and on and on. I couldn't see the end of it over the horizon, which made me suck in breaths and sob harder. There, under the watchful gaze of the Riviera sun, I would become the most timid me on record.

I had made a one-sided pact with God. One I felt he should endorse and certainly obey. Didn't God agree that my past was just too hard and that I needed a much happier, stress-free life? Even though theologically I knew this was the wrong sort of bargain to attempt to strike with God and that hard times plague everyone, I still *believed* he owed me peace in my circumstances. I didn't want to believe Jesus's words, "I have told you all this so that you may have peace in me. Here on earth you will have many trials and sorrows. But take heart, because I have overcome the world" (John 16:33).

I didn't want peace in trials. I wanted peace *from* trials.

But Jesus did not obey my wishes. Instead, he gave me Sadness Mountain, which morphed into an angry volcano that erupted all over me and my family.

So there I sat, blubbering between gut-wrenching sobs, fully aware that I would not improve, that depression lurked nearby, and that I had no way of remedying the situation. I certainly had no more guts. I was a church planter, a writer, a mother, a team member, a tentative friend, a language fumbler, a worship leader—all these things defined me during that time. But what was I really? A mess of a mess. Weaker than I'd ever been in the history of Mary.

I did not feel strong. Haunted by my extreme inadequacy, my husband despaired of me. I had been so capable in the United

States. So together. So happy. So with it. But take me to foreign soil, add language stress, church-planting team fights (there were several), children experiencing horrible trials in schools, financial woe in the form of selling our home in Texas to a con man and being forced to foreclose, an unknown sickness that rendered me bedridden many days, a few enemies, and the most concentrated and overt spiritual warfare our family had ever experienced, and you have me, powerless.

You may be in that place right now. You may feel utterly overwhelmed by life's blows that seem to come over and over and over again. You've heard that chaos comes in threes, but you stopped counting at twenty-seven. Your self-worth is broken beyond repair because you feel so beaten down and worthless.

I understand.

As I mentioned above, I scared my husband with my neediness. "I don't know who I am anymore," I cried. And, sadly, he agreed. He'd lost the go-getter wife who took on trials with gusto. She'd become a mouse of a woman—timid, shaking, preferring the cocoon of that tiny townhome to the French-speaking frenzy of life outside the front door.

Yet there are those promises peppered throughout the New Testament, aren't there? About our weakness being the very stage where Jesus does his best work.

- The Spirit helps us pray when we are weak (Rom. 8:26).
- God actually chooses the weak to shame the strong (1 Cor. 1:27).
- When we're weak, he is strong (2 Cor. 12:9–10).
- He is powerful among us (2 Cor. 13:3).
- Our weakness helps us lean into Jesus (2 Cor. 13:4).
- The heroes of the faith saw their weakness turned to strength (Heb. 11:34).

When we think of the apostle Paul, our first impression is lion-like strength. He was a formidable worker for Jesus, unafraid, powerful. But if you read through Paul's letters with a little less of a "can-do" filter and a lot more of a wide-open understanding of his humanity, you'll catch the irony. Paul wasn't as strong as we sometimes think he was. Trials overwhelmed him. Fears assailed his confidence. He despaired. He battled shipwrecks, sicknesses, a snakebite, verbal and physical lashings, and untold persecutions. Once he told the Corinthian believers, "I came to you in weakness—timid and trembling. And my message and my preaching were very plain. Rather than using clever and persuasive speeches, I relied only on the power of the Holy Spirit. I did this so you would trust not in human wisdom but in the power of God" (1 Cor. 2:3–5). Picture that: the great apostle Paul, timid and trembling!

In this crazy, upside-down world that prizes power over timidity, flash over faithfulness, and cleverness over plain talk, let it soak in that Paul possessed none of the former and all of the latter. Timid, faithful, plain-talking Paul.

In that living room, sitting on an uncomfortable chair, with head in my hands, I more resembled that rendition of the apostle Paul than the one I had conjured up in my head. And here's the strange truth: that time in France was the seedbed of death—death of dreams, death of what I thought I should be, death of ambition, death of my own personal strength. Jesus said, "I tell you the truth, unless a kernel of wheat is planted in the soil and dies, it remains alone. But its death will produce many new kernels—a plentiful harvest of new lives" (John 12:24). The paradox of the Christian life is that death precedes resurrection. Broken comes before healed, depression before the light.

I needed the fire of France to become the on-fire Jesus follower I am today. I could not see that Mary while the tears flowed. In fact, I shook my fist at God, wondering why in the world "what I always feared has happened to me. What I dreaded has come true" (Job 3:25). I could only see the death, the weakness. I could not foretell the growth, the depth, and the maturity that would come because of my weakness.

While this kind of weakness threatens to undermine our worth, instead, it should serve as a catalyst for longing. God never wastes our weakness. In fact, our weakness is the very place he does his most beautiful work. Paul knew this, most likely because he had been trained by weakness. He had learned to welcome it as a friend, knowing his weakened state would leave room for the power of God. I can imagine him rejoicing in James's wise words, "When all kinds of trials and temptations crowd into your lives my brothers, don't resent them as intruders, but welcome them as friends! Realise that they come to test your faith and to produce in you the quality of endurance" (James 1:2–3 Phillips).

Paul did more than welcome his weaknesses; he learned to boast about them. "Therefore, I have cheerfully made up my mind to be proud of my weaknesses, because they mean a deeper experience of the power of Christ" (2 Cor. 12:9 Phillips). He was proud of his weaknesses! What a strange, countercultural thought, particularly to the American way of thinking that's chock-full of buffed resolve, that praises the powerful and maligns the weak-willed. Paul learned the secret of boasting about his smallness. "If I must boast, I would rather boast about the things that show how weak I am. God, the Father of our Lord Jesus, who is worthy of eternal praise, knows I am not lying" (2 Cor. 11:30–31). In this passage, it's almost as if he's trying to prove to the Corinthian believers that he's telling the truth. He mentions God the Father to demonstrate his truthfulness.

It seems so strange to us. Why would Paul say it's awesome to be weak? Because frailty is the pathway to God's power. As we look at this paradox, consider four truths to internalize as you face your own weakness: you can make peace with your neediness, suffering doesn't negate your worth, those who bend the knee change the world, and living broken points to the broken Savior.

You Can Make Peace with Your Neediness

I have a different relationship with our cat, Scout, than I do our aging golden retriever, Pippin. Scout lives aloof. She doesn't need me, barely tolerates me if I'm being honest. And because of that, I chase her around wanting her to please, please love me. This has never worked. When she sees me, she runs for her life.

Pippin, on the other paw, needs me. He is neediness personified (dogified?). Because he can no longer stand up on his own, I have to lift his back haunches to get him to stand. He yelps. He moans. He breathes heavily. And when I leave the room, he lets out this particular high-pitched yelp that sets me on edge. I don't chase him. I don't pine for his loyalty and affection. In some ways, I resent him and, in my mind, tell him he's far too needy.

Maybe I chase Scout because aloof is safe. Aloof is what I value, what I want to be, what I wish I could be. And maybe I disdain Pippin because he reminds me of the part of me I've tried to squelch all these years. I despise my neediness. Hate it. Abhor it. Wish I would never be helpless or needy again.

Because when we're helpless and needy, we hope and sometimes demand that others fill the void. And if or when they don't, our neediness escalates, leaving us feeling emptier.

The utter fear of inconveniencing someone with my neediness has its roots in my childhood. It's most likely why I never told my parents about the sexual abuse when it was happening. I feared needing their attention, but more than that, I felt that if I revealed my inconvenient neediness, they might leave me, and I'd be left with a greater gaping wound. Or maybe I was afraid they'd do nothing with my confession. It's hard to figure out why I held back, but I decided it was safer for me to take the abuse than report it. When I look back at that poor little girl, violated and shaking, you'd think I'd have compassion on her. Instead, I despise her.

How dare she be so needy.

How dare she need others to help her.

How dare she inconvenience the adults in her life with her needs.

Yet that is precisely the opposite of how God sees me. And it's the opposite of how he views you. He created the human heart to be fulfilled in him alone. Because Jesus walked this worn-out earth, experiencing the detriments and pains of life, he can come alongside us and understand. However, we often fail to realize this. Instead, we try to force people to meet our needs. Sometimes we fashion another person into an idol—someone we bow down to when we're hurting—and if that person shuns us or grows weary of our neediness, our world implodes.

God's desire is that we see things clearly, that we shake hands with our very real neediness. Instead of demanding that others fill us up or even recognize our pain, we must first run to Jesus. He is the safest place to be when we are feeling needy. He does not despise it. He does not roll his sacred eyes when we once again approach the throne of grace. (Remember, his throne is not a throne of "I told you so" but of audacious love and open grace.) He is best qualified to meet our deepest needs, and he welcomes every part of us—particularly the needy bits.

In her book *Living without Jim*, my friend Sue Keddy recounts the days and months after the sudden, unexpected death of her missionary husband. She was forty-six years old when he sat next to her on the couch that morning. They were reading 2 Corinthians 12:9–10, quoted earlier, about God being strong in our weakness. Jim laughed. His eyes widened. Then a gurgling noise emitted from his throat. He died on the couch after suffering a massive heart attack, and no amount of CPR could revive him.

One of the things Sue learned after Jim's death was just how much she had relied on him in her life, how she had laid her fears and stresses at his feet. So as she grieved him, she realized her gigantic longing for Jesus—that she needed to run to him with her heart since Jim was no longer there. She writes, "I always believed I loved Jesus more than Jim, and in theory *maybe* that was true, but I'm realizing now that when I was freaking out and needed reassurance, it was Jim I ran to, not Jesus. We were a dynamic duo joined at the hip on a most incredible adventure that took us literally around the world."[1] In her grief, in her need, Sue had to learn to run first to Jesus. She writes, "I know that without the Lord's intervention, I'd be in a very dark place. It's so easy to entertain self-pity and live in the hollows of despair, so I'm thankful that when I call, *He comes.*"[2]

It's okay to be needy. God does not deride your neediness, and neither should you. Shake hands with it. Welcome it if you can. Because that place of terrible need is the launchpad of a beautiful life. Annihilation must precede resurrection. Need comes before filling. You're actually in the best place you've ever been spiritually when you're at your lowest. God rescues those who reach for him. He cannot rescue those who don't need him. Psalm 138:6 reminds us of who can be near God: "Though the LORD is great, he cares for the humble, but he keeps his distance from the proud."

Suffering Doesn't Negate Your Worth

I saved the document I typed in college about suffering. It's yellowed from age, and the typing is rife with errors, but I returned to that paper time and time again. The title? "Security, Suffering, Sovereignty." I wanted to mine the depths of the whys of suffering, understand Job and his heavy pain, and come to conclusions that were less than cliché. Because the truth is, when we suffer, the cliché chatter rises. But what do we sincerely need? Truth laced with hands-and-feet love. A settled belief that God is in the midst of our pain and woe and ire.

I found how joy, ironically, intertwined itself with suffering—a quirky and somewhat unwanted paradox. I quote Kenneth Caraway on the yellowing document: "There is no box made by God nor us but that the sides can be flattened out and the top blown off, to make a dance floor on which to celebrate life."[3] Celebrate suffering? Paul seemed to think so, as he wrote in Philippians, known as the joy epistle, which is bursting with pain intermingled with Paul's otherworldly joy. "Always be full of joy in the Lord. I say it again—rejoice! Let everyone see that you are considerate in all you do. Remember, the Lord is coming soon" (Phil. 4:4–5). In 1 Thessalonians 5:16–18, he reminds those who suffer to "always be joyful. Never stop praying. Be thankful in all circumstances, for this is God's will for you who belong to Christ Jesus."

Suffering becomes the darkened backdrop where redemption shines all the fiercer. It brings into focus the sharp contrast between evil and good, and it clarifies an eternal perspective for the believer. We are not made for this world but for one where wrongs are righted, tears are wiped away, and unending joy abounds.

That all looks pretty on paper, but real life is much more difficult. Especially when we think trials negate our worth. We think only those who are flawed or broken or messy merit the suffering life. Of course we'd never say that out loud. We know enough about evil in the world—the pestilence, genocide, discrimination, and heartache—to know that entering into a relationship with God doesn't change the world system. But deep down, we still believe that when we meet Jesus, roses and sunshine will follow, that we deserve a better life than the one we eked out without him. But Scripture does not support this type of health and wealth theology:

- "Yes, and everyone who wants to live a godly life in Christ Jesus will suffer persecution" (2 Tim. 3:12).
- "Dear friends, don't be surprised at the fiery trials you are going through, as if something strange were happening to you" (1 Pet. 4:12).
- "Do you remember what I told you? 'A slave is not greater than the master.' Since they persecuted me, naturally they will persecute you. And if they had listened to me, they would listen to you" (John 15:20).

Job's entire story shows that God, in his sovereignty, allows suffering. It doesn't mean God loved Job less, but it does show that God had a plan for him far beyond his understanding. Before, when he was blessed and had everything, he loved God. He heard God's voice. He even had a good grasp on the ways of God when he said, "I came naked from my mother's womb, and I will be naked when I leave. The LORD gave me what I had, and the LORD has taken it away. Praise the name of the LORD!" (Job 1:21). Even after everything went awry, Job spoke these profound words. What followed? Chapter after chapter of grief as he worked through the losses.

After he suffered and learned to grieve, his relationship with God deepened. As pain trained him, he realized his smallness in the bigness of God's greatness—and even so, he began to truly, deeply, and wonderfully *experience* his powerful God. He said, "I had only heard about you before, but now I have seen you with my own eyes" (Job 42:5).

It reminds me of a story I recently read about a woman named Ema McKinley who spent most of her adult life bent sideways over a wheelchair, her back crooked as a result of a traumatic accident and resulting health condition called RSD (reflex sympathetic dystrophy), one of the most painful physical conditions a person can endure. After eighteen years of unending pain and disfigurement, Ema fell out of her wheelchair on Christmas Eve. Jesus appeared in her office where she lay and healed her crooked body. When her sons and grandsons discovered her the next day, she scared them all by walking upright, no longer crooked and without her wheelchair.

This documented miracle amazed Ema and the people around her. In one of her first speaking engagements after the profound healing, she told a group of men in an addiction program:

> You don't ever want to give up. Oh, my goodness, people. Jesus is so real. Make him part of your day. Talk to him. Build a relationship with him. I don't know anybody who could stand up to that level of pain and suffering without him. You just can't. That kind of strength comes only from Jesus. It comes from asking him and trusting him every single day. Sometimes our hearts are literally broken with pain. But let me tell you, precious people, there's only one person who can mend a shattered heart, and that's Jesus. Call on him as your lifetime friend. He'll never leave you.[4]

Suffering ushered Ema into a deeper relationship with Jesus. It didn't undermine her worth, though I'm sure many days she wondered if God actually loved her because of the trials after trials she experienced. As a good parent, God disciplines those he loves (Prov. 3:12; Heb. 12:6; Rev. 3:19). But also like a good parent, he walks with us through the pain.

"Now I have proof that you hate me," I yelled in the car on the way to the hospital.[5] Face wet with tears, diaphragm aching from all the heaving, twenty-four-year-old me had operated under the assumption that God owed me a perfect life. Since I had already endured Job-like trials as a child, certainly God would lighten up and keep my adulthood agony-free. Newly pregnant and overjoyed at building a family from the wreckage of my own, I lost my breath when the doctor said he couldn't find a baby in my uterus. "Are you sure you're pregnant?" he asked.

The sickness said yes. The blue line said yes. But my womb said no.

After hours of surgery, the truth emerged—ectopic pregnancy, with no guarantee it wouldn't happen again. I wondered if I'd ever have children. The darkness overshadowed me, pushing me toward despair.

God hadn't conformed to my plans. He had allowed me to lose that pregnancy and endure surgery, which, in my pain-streaked mind, meant he simply did not love me. Good plans? To prosper and not harm me? Hogwash. I shrunk inside myself, cried creeks, rivers, lakes, oceans, all while I struggled with what seemed to be a capricious and arbitrary God who favored others over me, particularly any other woman whose baby bump mocked my lack of one.

I experienced my own Job journey. I eventually could say the words about giving and taking away, blessing him anyway. On the other end of the grief, I saw God more keenly than I had perceived him before. I developed a deeper understanding of those who suffer, a heightened awareness of the sufferings of Jesus, and I grew more grateful that I had a God who pursued me, shouldered my grief, and could handle my very stark now-I-know-you-hate-me words in the car. Like Peter, I could say, "Lord, to whom would we go? You have the words that give eternal life" (John 6:68).

I learned that suffering didn't undermine my worth—it eventually solidified it. God chased me through the pain. I reached for him through it. And I found him capable of bearing the weight of my anger, confusion, and raw-honest musings. Emptied of my expectations (how I thought my life should be), I could go to God with an unfilled cup so he could fill it. Tim Hansel wrote, "Only empty hands can receive. Pain is only another road to wisdom."[6]

God's attention to us during our suffering proves we are worthy. His love is available to us, particularly when trials and pains overwhelm us. His is a love of presence, according to Bob Goff.

> The world can make you think love can be picked up at a garage sale or enveloped in a Hallmark card. But the kind of love that God created and demonstrated is a costly one because it involves sacrifice and presence. It's a love that operates more like sign language than being spoken outright . . . The brand of love Jesus offers is. . . . more about presence than undertaking a project. It's a brand of love that doesn't just think about good things, or agree with them, or talk about them. . . . Love Does.[7]

Those Who Bend the Knee Change the World

When we think of powerhouses of the faith, we tend to picture warriors, people standing up to enemies. Martyrs even. But truly, the ones who change the world do so from their knees, in a posture of humility. Consider those who kneel in the New Testament:

- a demon-possessed man (Mark 5:6)
- Jairus, whose daughter was dying (Mark 5:22–23)
- a man whose son had seizures (Matt. 17:14)
- a man with leprosy (Mark 1:40)
- a Greek woman whose daughter had an unclean spirit (Mark 7:25)
- Mary, the sister of Lazarus, after his death (John 11:32)
- a woman who desperately wanted to anoint Jesus (Luke 7:38)

These people personified desperation. Death, disease, and demons marked the first six of these interactions. Have you faced death? Has a friend or loved one neared death's door? Have you been sick? Has someone else's sickness left you sad, needy, and feeling vulnerable? Have you battled a demonic attack? Have you seen friends or family wrestle with demons?

If you have, you've no doubt felt the weight of helplessness and despair. In those times, you have two choices: give in to the feelings or give your fear to God. These folks chose the latter. They didn't care how foolish they looked to others. They chose to humble themselves at great personal cost. They simply, desperately needed Jesus.

I simply, desperately need Jesus.

You simply, desperately need Jesus.

In that place of brokenness, I've experienced the presence of Jesus like never before. This type of experience tends to happen when everything else is cast aside, replaced by the deep, deep longing for the One who will truly satisfy. I've been in that place the past year. Truth be told, I've chosen to kneel before many other things.

- I thought success would fill me, but even when I received an accolade, I needed more applause to satiate me.
- I thought perfect relationships would satisfy, only to see them shift, some becoming painful, some distant.
- I thought if I had provision in a certain dollar amount, I'd finally have peace. But money is a fickle mistress. It shapeshifts so that you always feel you "need" more to be happy. It's an illusion.
- I worshiped at the altar of getting things done, only to have the items on my to-do list multiply like bunnies in springtime.

Sometimes I've felt like God has held back success from me to teach me dependence, to keep me in the place of surrender and brokenness. He is training me to always give him the glory for any shred of success. Believe me, I'm learning. I'm seeing. I'm finally understanding.

My desperation hasn't always made me kneel. Sometimes it has made me bitter. Have you experienced feelings of bitterness too? Where you blame God for not abiding by your agenda? For not meeting your expectations? It's normal, but it's costly to your soul. Eventually, bitterness makes you sour-faced and sour-hearted. Is that the life you want?

One day at church a relational burden I had been carrying a long time pressed in on me. It felt like I was suffocating, grieving, and panicking all while being wrapped up in pain. I began worshiping God during the song "At the Cross" by Chris Tomlin. No tears, but oh how they threatened. When the lyrics spoke of bowing down, I sensed God asking me to obey the words I sang to him. This was not comfortable to me in our big church, as I was standing near the aisle and the only real way to kneel was to scoot a bit into the walkway. No one else did such a nutty thing, but I've come to the place in my walk with Jesus that I know I'd rather look dorky or foolish than disobey him. So I knelt. And then I cried.

Deep, dark, painful tears. All the weight of that burden I'd been carrying flushed from me. I pleaded with God about the pain I carried, asked him what to do.

His response? "Mary, love me," he said. So I continued the song on my knees, feeling awkward but met by Jesus. My husband was late in getting to church, but my college-aged daughter was there, her hand resting on my shoulder. And as I continued to cry, another hand, my husband's, touched the other shoulder. In that circle of three, I sensed God's peace.

All that to say, sometimes we don't realize the burdens we're carrying until we bow, until we kneel, until we meet with Jesus in the dust. Please, please, if you are carrying a heavy load today, place your knees to the ground and pour your heart out to Jesus. Oh how he longs to relieve you, to unburden what you carry in your own strength. You will learn that the beauty of the broken place is that those times are the times we are nearly forced to reach for Jesus. That's a benefit because Jesus is our greatest benefit. When life seems fine, we coast along without him. But when we hurt, we reach.

Jesus meets us when everything else fails us, including the bitterness we cling to.

I could end the story here. You'd walk away reminding yourself to get on your knees today, giving everything to Jesus. And that would be a good thing. Physically kneeling brings understanding of our desperation for our Creator.

But I'd forget to discuss the woman from Luke 7 who desperately wanted to bless Jesus. She wasn't desperate for herself; she was captured by the unrelenting need to make him happy. She knelt before him because she wanted him to know how much she loved him.

I wish I could be more like her. Do you? To kneel because we desperately want Jesus to know how deeply and affectionately we love him? To be called a friend of God? As one who is after his heart? To be one he entrusts his secrets to because we've developed such a deep relationship?

Yeah, that. I want that.

{Pause}

I just returned from my knees. I prayed, "Jesus, I don't just want to be desperate. I want to be desperate for your presence in my life. I want to be your friend. I want to bless you." May that be our prayer today. Tomorrow. The next day. Let's be desperate for his acclaim. His honor. His affection.

Living Broken Points to the Broken Savior

I once listened to a new-to-me worship song. As the music washed over me, I felt the presence of Jesus. Enough to make me tear up.

My conversation with Jesus went something like this: "Lord, I'm tired of living with stress. Tired of feeling the repercussions of failure. Can't you make everything easier?"

"If I do, would you need me?"

I let that sink in. Maybe the reason trials topple on me (and you) is so we will have dependency instead of self-sufficiency. So that we'll need Jesus.

Peace settled over me like a fuzzy blanket on a shivery night.

And then, these words: "Live broken."

Though I admit this bit of heavenly advice is wise, I don't much like it. I'd rather live whole. Complete. Without worry or stress or painful situations. Without relational discord. Without irksome misunderstandings. Without heartache.

But then where would I be? Happily self-absorbed.

It reminds me of a quote I once found in *Streams in the Desert*:

> My dear God, I have never thanked You for my thorns. I have thanked You a thousand times for my roses, but not once for my thorns. I have always looked forward to the place where I will be rewarded for my cross, but I have never thought of my cross as a present glory itself. Teach me, O Lord, to glory in my cross. Teach me the value of my thorns. Show me how I have climbed to You through the path of pain. Show me it is through my tears I have seen my rainbows.[8]

It's true. It's in those broken places where I've been pierced by thorns that I understand where my sufficiency lies. In Jesus.

What if instead of berating ourselves for our failures and sins and besetting weaknesses, we remember that the sweetness of God informs our worth? What if instead of thinking, *God must be angry at me for all my struggles*, we think, *I am utterly grateful that he sees me as his beloved child. Nothing I do or don't do can change his great affection for me.*

This way of thinking is a game changer for me because my pattern when I've failed has been to knock myself over the head, yell at myself like an angry, out-of-control coach, and offer myself no grace.

Who behaves like that? Is that like God? Would he do that?

Of course he disciplines us. Of course he loves us too much to let us flounder in our mess. But all that discipline comes from a cheering heart and a desire to actually *empower* us in our weaknesses. Our weaknesses then become a dance floor for him to dance his steps.

Satan, the enemy of our souls, wants to knock us down, brutalize our thoughts, make us feel small and petty and awful. He thrives when we give in to this bullying. He comes to steal, kill, and destroy us. And our weakness and sin are open doorways for him to capitalize on us. When we give in to that shaming voice again and again and again and again, the things it says become the truth (even if they're a lie) that we believe like gospel.

We are unworthy.

We will never change.

Our sins define us forever.

We are bound to live in shame, shackled to it indefinitely.

Beautiful truth: God functions best in your weakness. It's the most amazing place for him to work his miracles. So instead of beating yourself up over your mess, just admit it. In so doing, you diffuse the worth-killing voices in your head and usher in God's bigness and strength.

....

TRUTH:

God's Best Work Is Done in Me When I'm Weak.

....

Questions for Reflection or Discussion

1. Why is it hard to consider that weakness has benefits?

2. What about our culture rallies against weakness?

3. What would it look like for you to make peace with your neediness? Or how would this look in a loved one's life?

4. Who has been a great example to you of letting God's strength shine through weakness?

5. When was the last time you felt that suffering negated your worth? Have you had an experience in which you truly understood your worth despite your suffering? What happened?

6. When was the last time you bent your knee and asked for God's help amid an overwhelming situation? (Or are you in a situation like that right now?) What was the result of kneeling?

7. What would it look like (and how would it be different) if you lived broken this next week?

—————————— WORTH PRAYER ——————————

Jesus, I blew it. I'm sorry. In fact, I'm sorry I keep blowing it. But I'm tired of tossing myself under the bus when I do. So this time would you please rescue me from the shaming bus? Would you show me that you love me, that you will renew me, that you will protect me? I choose to believe the truth today that you are for me. Instead of hitting myself repeatedly when I fall down, let me listen to your cheerleading voice. In no way does this diminish my need to repent. Nor does it mean I take sin casually. No. It simply means I am changing the way I deal with the aftermath of my confessed sin. I am resting in your great affection, just as my children can rest in knowing my love for them is constant. Take away the shame. Take away the depressive thoughts. Take away the feeling that I'm not worth your love. Replace all those things with the truth of your love. Amen.

6

I Am Secure

Because God has made us for himself, our hearts are restless until they rest in him.

Augustine of Hippo

. . . .

LIE:
Insecurity Will Always Define Me.

. . . .

I try desperately not to be one of those people who always peddle their wares to everyone. I don't want to be "that girl." I've been frustrated by people who use their friendships to up their multilevel marketing prowess or leverage their relationships to financially better themselves. I'm not sure why this bothers me so much—no doubt some sort of flaw in me—but the fear that I will be a pushy book saleswoman is very near to me.

I attended a women's conference just as my book *Not Marked: Finding Hope and Healing after Sexual Abuse* released. I brought a box of fifty books and asked Jesus to please show me who to give them to. But as the box waited, untouched, under the table where I sat, my insecurity roared to life. *You'll just be bothering people with your book. You'll appear self-serving. No one wants to receive a book like that, especially because of the subject matter. Don't appear to be capitalizing on this event, or people will think differently of you. Just put the books away and stop trying so hard.*

However, the box was heavy, and the last thing I wanted to do was lug it back to the car. So I swallowed my insecurity and began handing out the books. I fought fear the entire time, while I internally debated with myself. *Who will I give them to? Should I hide them, and if someone asks for one, then that will mean I should give it to them? Do I run around trying to find "influential" leaders to give one to? Wouldn't that be un-Jesusy (meaning, shouldn't I concentrate on giving them to anyone, regardless of influence)?*

So I battled myself. And insecurity won.

Thankfully, a few folks I knew actually did ask for the book. But then I found myself falling into a weird panic mode, wondering if hawking the books was wrong and worrying whether they would get in the "correct" hands. Sometimes, with a book in my hand, I stood to the side of people having conversations, waiting for a break to give it away. Nearly 100 percent of the people I gave a book to responded with a huge thank-you, but my insecurity prevented me from receiving their gratitude. Instead, I thought, *I am totally bothering this person. She's just being polite. She's important. Who am I to interrupt?*

Twice I saw my gift discarded on a table, causing feelings of unworthiness to creep into my skin. *You see? You have bothered people with your book. They really don't want it.*

All I wanted to do was give away copies of my book. But I ended up with a severe case of smallness. Some people call me brave. I just feel scaredy-cat obedient. I truly felt God wanted me to write that painful book. So I did. And now it was alive and well. Out there. In the hands of women who may toss it in the trash. Toss me in the trash.

Even so, even amid my titanic insecurity, I'm glad I went through the stressful exercise. It reminds me of who is God, who holds control, who ultimately gets the glory.

You see? When I'm smaller than a molecule, he is greater than a mountain. When I step aside, he steps in. When I shrink into insignificance, I make room for his genuine significance. When I stumble in awkwardness, he strengthens in hope.

We are all like the apostle Peter, boldly beginning our ministries (*I will write that book!*), stepping out of the boat of safety. But when our foot hits the waves, we falter (*What in the world have I done? Who am I?*). We begin to sink. We catch the eyes of our Savior, hoping he won't see our fear, our lack of faith, our failure. But he sees all of it. And instead of letting us slip beneath the bubbling wake, he reaches that beautiful work-worn hand our way, offers his grip, and rescues us.

We are insecure.

He is secure.

Yes, Jesus loves me.

Yes, Jesus loves you.

Insecure me. Insecure you. Messy me. Messy you. Small me. Small you. Worried me. Worried you.

You may not be peddling books at a conference while battling the insecurity beast, but I'm guessing you can relate in other ways. I suspect that you hear the same kind of voices in your head hollering your unworthiness, bolstering your insecurity. This goes to show that we, as women, often trust a fallacy—that all the other women in the world have it all together, whatever "it" may mean. Everyone else is secure and joyful and fulfilled and worthy.

But us?

We are flawed.

Except that we are all insecure, aren't we? The world does a bang-up job of reinforcing this to us, belittling our bodies, shaming our age, diminishing our successes, showing us that we'll never measure up to that yardstick. We tend to elevate others' security and amplify our own insecurity, when, in truth, we're all insecure. And the only true secure one is Jesus.

Tim Hansel wrote this a long time ago in the now out-of-print book *You Gotta Keep Dancing*. "If our security is based on something that can be taken away from us, we will constantly be living on the false edge of security."[1] In order to settle our worth, we must find the true edge of security. Hint: it lies in the person of Jesus Christ. Here are eight truths to help you find that kind of bedrock security.

1. God Wants to Remedy Your Identity

We have an identity crisis. We believe our identity lies in our sinful behavior or stellar performance, or that it's based wholly on our abilities. The solution to this kind of identity crisis is finding our identity in Christ. I've touched on this truth throughout the book—our worth is found in the incomparable Christ. He purchased our lives on the cross, welcoming us into his family. We are now the church, a bride, a holy priesthood, a child. As family members, our identity comes from whose we are, not who we are. And because Jesus's death and resurrection are historical, completed acts, there is no room for insecurity. We cannot undo his sacrifice. It is settled and accomplished.

When we forget our identity in Christ, we heap a load of shame on ourselves for not measuring up to impossible standards. We live as if our identity depends on our behavior. But the only behavior our identity is based on is the loving acts of Jesus. That's why faith is important—believing what Jesus did exceeds our very best day of living. His perfection settles our worth, which means our imperfection cannot unsettle it.

2. God's Love for You Is a Bedrock Truth

My friend Sarah has a compelling perspective that maybe you've struggled with too. I know I have. She writes:

> When I was a child, I had vivid dreams, though I was often still awake. Small creatures—I could not tell you what they were, minions of some sort—would chase around in my head. Round and round and round, faster and faster, spinning in my mind until I was dizzy and shaking my head trying to make them stop. I was tortured by these waking dreams for many years. I had never heard of Jesus, but I always cried out for help. I knew there was Someone who could make it stop. At twelve, my brother told me about the Lord. He had just become a Christian and used the Romans Road tract to lead me into my new relationship with God. The part I remember the most about [the tract] was learning I was a sinner, I was bad, and I was never good enough for God. I accepted these things as truth and followed the tract's instructions and prayed that prayer. Now I was accepted by God. Now he could look on me and walk with me, but before, he couldn't, wouldn't.
>
> It saddens me when I think of that day. It was a good day in many senses, but a lie was implanted in me, and it grew. The lie I believed said I wasn't worth God's time back when I was a child crying out to him because I didn't know his name. That he didn't care about me until I cared about him. My throat tightens and my eyes fill with tears as I write these words.[2]

What Sarah is saying is that she felt God could love her only if she was already his, that she was somehow damaged or dirty beforehand and, therefore, intrinsically unworthy of his love. This view says, "God loves those who are lovable, and that's it." But the truth is Jesus died for you and for me—before we were even conceived, before our parents, grandparents, great-grandparents yowled their way into this world. God exists outside time and space as we know it, and his love and sacrifice are settled. They are based on his goodness, not ours. He loves us when we are far from him. He loves us when we're near. He loved us when we didn't know him, and he loves us when we do.

3. God Defines Your Security, and Criticism from Others Can't Shake It

Unlike skilled salespeople who have learned that a rejection of their product does not equal a rejection of them, I have not quite internalized that fact. Every criticism feels like a rejection of me. When someone is critical of me, it throws me into a sad eddy of feeling worthless. Since I wrongly equate my worth with either what I do or what people think of me, criticism becomes a double-edged sword of crabbiness.

I sense I'm on the cusp of something brand spanking new, a revival of sorts. But deeper than that, I feel a strengthening of my innards, a holy confidence that I've longed for but seldom reached (those pesky insecurities and battles with worth run deep, deep, deep). And yet, if I step out, grow into my own skin, be wildly and wholly loved by Jesus, which I then reflect in how I live, the enemy of my soul (and yours) will *not* like that. He'll throw things my (your) way.

What has been your reaction when others have criticized you?

Francis Frangipane seems to get it. He writes, "If you are going to be successful in the Lord's work, you must find God's hiding place from one of the most painful weapons in Satan's arsenal: the critical tongue."[3] Can I hear an *amen*? Psalm 31:20 confirms Frangipane's words: "You hide them in the shelter of your presence, safe from those who conspire against them. You shelter them in your presence, far from accusing tongues." God is the One who shelters us. When those critical tongues flap our way, we must take that opportunity to flee to his presence, asking him to sift us, to help us sort out the hurtful words, and to heal our word wounds.

Simply being aware of Satan's schemes has helped me tremendously—particularly when I'm on the cusp of renewal and an internal revival. Frangipane clarifies, "It is while the new work of God is trembling forward that Satan seeks to bring his greatest assault. The form he takes in his war against our new beginnings in Christ is accusation."[4] So if you're experiencing an unusual amount of criticism from others, take heart. It need not undercut your security in Christ or your feelings of worth. Attack may mean you're on the brink of spiritual breakthrough. That's encouraging!

Frangipane shares about a time in his ministry when criticism felt unrelenting. God didn't remove the critical people. Instead, God used that very criticism to change him. Criticism can be like the thorn in apostle Paul's flesh, given to us by God to keep us from exalting ourselves and to force us to truly, deeply rely on Jesus for true worth and shelter. Frangipane writes, "To inoculate me from the praise of man, He baptized me in the criticism of man until I died to the control of man."[5] Yes. This. Yes.

I'm feeling the weight and beauty of that in my life right now. A letting go of the words spoken against me. A pressing into the God who is more after my holiness than my happiness. A carving away of my insatiable need for approval. A more settled place where I feel comfortable in my skin, finally.

It's tyranny when we live for the applause or approval of everyone. And when we dare to step out, walk in newness and freedom, be assured criticism will come.

4. Satan Hates Free Christians

Hates them.

He wants us enslaved to the approval of others, to become immobilized after receiving criticism, introspective to a fault. So he often uses people to hurl hurt our way. And here's the kicker: they are often Christians. This makes the whole mess a powerful mixture of fear and craziness and confusion. We don't have to live in this mess. We don't have to let those who criticize us upset us for weeks and months. The simple solution is to use the criticism to catapult us toward Jesus. Because Jesus gets it. He was misunderstood. Maligned. Called a demon (can you imagine?). He comes to us in the fear and loathing that arise in the aftermath of criticism.

Frangipane continues, "As much as I hated it when people slandered me, this was the very thing God used to compel me nearer to His heart."[6] So instead of being undermined when criticized, be fruitful. Instead of mulling over the criticism, give it to Jesus to sort through. Instead of letting it stop you in your tracks, dare to take another step toward your dream. Don't let the criticism deter you.

Important note: I'm not advocating we never listen to criticism or heed it. Wise people listen to it and take it to heart. But it doesn't need to infect your soul like poison. Give it to Jesus, find joy, and move on.

5. God Sees When Others Misunderstand Your Heart

I got a call from a number I didn't recognize. I answered. On the other end was a tax official. She spent several minutes insinuating something about me that was untrue. It really bothered me. More than I care to admit. Later it occurred to me that this woman and her words rattled something deeper. It unsettled my heart. Why?

Because I value integrity. I love doing the right thing, even when no one's watching. I have a healthy fear of wrongdoing, and I'm passionate about being a good citizen, law abider, friend, worker.

The insinuations reminded me of another time when a friend completely misread my heart. The repercussions of her words still hurt. Deeply. During the situation, I realized quickly that nothing I could say would convince her of my heart or prove my innocence. So I stopped trying to convince her. I cried out to Jesus instead. I gave my reputation to him to manage. I remember the release I felt when I realized this truth about God: he sees.

He sees your heart. He sees your motives (and there are plenty of impure ones mixed together in a jumble of confusion and integrity in mine). He sees the bureaucrat's heart. He discerns a friend's heart. He knows our desires. It's completely freeing to know that even if someone else doesn't believe us, we don't need to "protest too much." We can rest. God sees. He knows. He rewards those who are faithful.

This is a reminder not to pass judgment on someone's motives and heart or accuse blindly or jump to conclusions without patiently listening and asking questions or not to become bitter before we have a chance to forgive. Bitterness, if we let it take root, does an awful thing. It makes us blind to a person's heart. It assigns negative intent to that person. It sees only the bad and is oblivious to the good.

Far too many times in my life I've listened to gossip about someone else. If that's the first thing I hear about them, then it forever colors my view of them. The older and wiser I get, the less I give weight to the first piece of information I hear. I try to meet a person fresh, try to draw them out and discover their heart. Not always, but I try.

Because I know how painful it is to be misunderstood.

I thank Jesus, though, that he truly understands what it's like to be misunderstood and judged wrongly, to have others insinuate things about you. Consider this: "But Jesus on his part did not entrust himself to them, because he knew all people and needed no one to bear witness about man, for he himself knew what was in man" (John 2:24–25 ESV). He let God the Father hold his reputation. He understood the fickleness of crowds. He felt the weight of their judgments, which ultimately led to his death.

So if others are insinuating things about you, press into Jesus. Give him your worries and fears. He can shoulder such things. He understands.

6. You Are Never Alone Even When You Feel Lonely

My daughter Julia and I ascended the high overpass crossing from one behemoth Texas freeway to another. I usually love the climb, as it's the only time I have a mountain-like perspective in Texas, a land (at least where I live) of little topography. But this time, in the corner of my periphery, I spied a black clump on the cement guardrail to my right. I slowed slightly, keeping an eye out for the car behind me. In a split second, the clump morphed into a frightened black and white kitten, mewing on the apex of the overpass. I cringed, then gasped. There was no shoulder, and the car behind me kept advancing. If I stopped, I would endanger my life, my daughter's life, and the lives of any others who might slam into me.

I had to keep driving.

But I've been haunted by that kitten ever since.

Julia and I prayed that God would rescue the mewing kitten, and I sure hope he did.

The thing is I think we have all felt like that kitten. There have been times in our lives when the decisions of another person left us stranded in a scary place, a place not of our choosing. And the world whirs by, either unable or unwilling to help. We mew our fear. We shake. We beg wide-eyed for rescue, but nothing happens.

And in that place, we are alone. Or at least we feel that way.

Maybe you feel that way right now.

Maybe you're sitting, frightened, on a guardrail way up high, with no rescue in sight. You need a friend to stop the car and gently guide you to safety. You need to know God sees you there, but you also need a helping hand. I've found that the isolating life of a writer has hindered my security because I have no one during the day with whom to process my thoughts. I live too much in my head. When that happens, my thinking tends to spiral.

God created the body of Christ to rescue us, to listen to our worries, to reassure us, to help us. When we become too isolated, we give in to destructive thoughts. My mom used to notice when I grew too stir-crazy in the house, playing alone with dolls, talking to my imaginary friend. She would say, "Go outside and blow your stink off," which really meant that I needed to leave the house and interact with other people my own age.

7. Security Is Based on the Bigness of God, Not the Smallness of You

Have you ever given in to panic? Boy howdy, I have. And it leads to fear-mongering and sin. Once, during a particularly vexing time when I faced an enemy of sorts, I panicked, retaliated in kind, and made a mess of things. My panic gave my "enemy" more fuel to hate me. Not a fun encounter, to be sure.

So I get panic.

I do panic.

I've languished in the land of panic.

But I don't want to give in to panic as I have in the past. Thankfully, God offers a principle—a secret—to help us overcome panic: resting in his deliverance. And for that, we can look to Gideon from Old Testament fame—the reluctant commander who would eventually deliver Israel from its enemies. Gideon isn't much of a poster child for a less-panicked life. He didn't recognize the Angel of the Lord right away, called him "sir." And he asked for signs right and left to make sure it was God who spoke to him. Prone to panic, he was.

But he learned a secret.

God acts on our behalf when circumstances seem impossible.

Stop and reread that sentence. Let it sink into your bones.

With only three hundred men, Gideon routed thousands and thousands of enemies because God fought for them. "When the 300 Israelites blew their rams' horns, the Lord caused the warriors in the camp to fight against each other with their swords" (Judg. 7:22). The result? Peace—not panic. "Throughout the rest of Gideon's lifetime—about forty years—there was peace in the land" (Judg. 8:28). We can have peace. We don't need to give in to panic. God acts broadly on our behalf, particularly when the impossible looms.

8. Security Depends on Attachment

It's a thread I don't want to see, but God seems to align the signs like Hansel and Gretel bread crumbs. While reading an article about a child thrashing around due to reactive attachment disorder, I freeze. She is me. I am her. I understand more than I wish to. I highlight a quote: "Because their needs were met so randomly when they were young, they believe the only ones they can trust are themselves. The notion of intimacy is particularly threatening.

If I let someone get close to me, they will hurt me. It is easier to stay in control, at a safe distance."[7]

And although I've done a lot of work to accept the past and have addressed my hyperactive fear of abandonment, I resonate far too deeply with these sentences about control and distance. And then these words: "Her greatest accomplishment is letting love in."

The events of my early childhood attest to my struggles. Because of circumstances outside her control, my mom retracted from me, too young and perhaps too immature to understand the needs of a baby. I didn't feel soothed, loved, cared for. As I analyze my childhood, I see signs of attachment problems. I'd hyper attach to some, disregard others. I lived in a state of constant vigilance, never letting my guard down because, if I did, I could not save myself. I never, ever felt that the adults in my life had my best interest in mind, or even had me in mind at all. Instead, I was in the way, an unwelcomed add-on to their lives. Why bother with that little nuisance girl?

I seemed to be hardwired to be abandoned by others. Couple that with a penchant for hypochondria and drama, and you had a young girl who longed for attention and got little. I had an unhealthy addiction to chaos, a need for things to be difficult in order to feel sane. (This permeates my life even today. If life seems normal, I get edgy.) As I look at the list of symptoms of attachment disorder, I see I am not a clear-cut case. And I'm amazed that Jesus has healed so much of me, that I'm not wholeheartedly detached from the human race.

As I type this, I'm very aware of my own shortcomings as a parent. I, no doubt, brought my broken self into parenthood, and there are times I'm sure I hurt my children by not responding quickly to their needs. It makes my heart ache to think of that, but it reminds me of something a friend shared with me a long time ago that has stuck with me. She said, "If we are everything to our children, then they will never need Jesus." In my frailty, I've left plenty of room for Jesus.

And, honestly, I'm to the point where I'm grateful for my childhood. Oddly so. Because of how I felt, I had a gaping need for love and found that love in Jesus. I've clung to him. I've needed him. I've attached myself to him. And I've found him to be trustworthy and good.

But that's not the entire story. Because some days I wonder if God really is good, if he is trustworthy. Today, for example, I am mining the depths of the kind of sadness that comes when loved ones stray from Christ. I wonder, *Is it really true that Jesus pursues everyone? Does he really love us all? Or does he play favorites? Does he attach only to the pious ones? The correct ones? Does he truly chase the one and leave the ninety-nine?*

This makes me think of the patriarch Jacob, whose name means "grabber of the heel," and how he spent his life attached to the lure of the firstborn rights yet detached from God Almighty. He learned to live scrappy, MacGyvering his way through life, finagling and finessing his future. And later, as he prepared to meet his betrayed brother, Esau, on the plains, he spent an exhausting night wrestling with God. To stop Jacob's tenacity, the one he wrestled against messed with his hip, detaching sinew from bone so that Jacob, who was proud and independent, limped for the rest of his life.

"Then Jacob asked, 'Please tell me your name.' 'Why do you ask my name?' the man replied. Then he blessed Jacob there. So Jacob named the place Peniel, explaining, 'Certainly I have seen God face to face and have survived.' The sun rose over him as he crossed over Penuel, but he was limping because of his hip" (Gen. 32:29–31 NET).

Jacob left the encounter with a limp and a legacy—a new name, which means "prevails with God." (See Gen. 32:22–32.) From a supplanter of authority to a submitter to God's authority. From schemer to wrestler to patriarch. While he may once have been guilty of spiritual detachment disorder, he now had a gimpy hip to remind him of his connection to God. Our level of security directly compares to our connection to God. See how beautifully God restored Jacob and his ancestors?

> But now, listen to me, Jacob my servant,
> Israel my chosen one.
> The LORD who made you and helps you says:
> Do not be afraid, O Jacob, my servant,
> O dear Israel, my chosen one.
> For I will pour out water to quench your thirst
> and to irrigate your parched fields.
> And I will pour out my Spirit on your descendants,
> and my blessing on your children.
> They will thrive like watered grass,
> like willows on a riverbank.
> Some will proudly claim, "I belong to the LORD."
> Others will say, "I am a descendant of Jacob."
> Some will write the LORD's name on their hands
> and will take the name of Israel as their own.
> Isaiah 44:1–5

If you're drowning in insecurity, perhaps it's time to write the Lord's name on your hand as a sign of your attachment to him. Not permanently (although I've done this with the word *Jesus* on my wrist), but temporarily as a reminder of whose you are.

Insecurity means three things—a lack of confidence, a lack of assurance, and a bucketful of self-doubt. Jesus remedies each. He will complete what he has started in us (Phil. 1:6). He assures us of our eternal destination (1 John 5:11–13). He strengthens us when we doubt ourselves (2 Cor. 12:9–10). Our security is based on something that cannot be taken away from us—Jesus Christ.

· ·

TRUTH:
Attaching to Jesus
Solidifies My Worth.

· ·

Questions for Reflection or Discussion

1. When has your security been based on something that can be taken away? What did you learn from that experience?

2. In the past five years, how has God remedied your identity? How does knowing your identity is secure in Christ help you face what's next?

3. When has criticism made you feel insecure? What did you do about the situation? What truths help you remember that your worth isn't based on someone else's opinion of you?

4. How does knowing that Jesus was misunderstood help you cope when you are misunderstood? When was the last time you placed your reputation in his hands and did not defend yourself? What happened?

5. How has loneliness undermined your security? When has sharing your feelings of insecurity with a friend helped you see things differently?

6. Would the person with whom you have the closest relationship describe you as insecure or secure? Why?

7. What makes you afraid to attach to others? To Jesus?

———————————— **WORTH PRAYER** ————————————

Jesus, you are my security. That is the truth. But so often I run to myself, my efforts, or the opinions of others to define me. Help me have confidence in your opinion of me. I want to be a woman who weathers criticism well, who chooses not to retaliate but to entrust myself to you. Help me not chase after insecure things. Please remedy my identity. Bring relationships into my life when loneliness reigns. I want to be attached to you more today than I've been in the past. Teach me what that means so I can truly rest securely in your embrace. Amen.

7

I Am Beautiful

You can take no credit for beauty at sixteen. But if you are beautiful at sixty, it will be your soul's own doing.

Marie Stopes

I stand in the scratchy grass of autumn in Texas and look at my feet again, thinking about why I'm here on earth and why lately I've been consumed with how I look and how sad that's made me feel. If I'm really honest, I have to admit that I hate what I see in the mirror, where cleverly designed clothes can't erase the years my body has walked on this earth. Stretch marks (well earned), extra stomach (too much bread), thighs that used to have the enviable

115

"thigh gap" now meet in the middle, strands of gray hair, heavy-laden eyelids. I am not what I used to be.

Except that I wasn't happy then either.

And now that I see pictures of me from when I was in my twenties, I want to grab that perky-looking twentysomething and shake her, hollering, "Do you know how good you have it? Just be grateful! You are beautiful."

But I cannot afford that grace, and I certainly don't grant it to my aging self today.

Have you ever felt this way?

Have you ever equated worth with how you look or how others look at you?

As I stand in the grass, it makes my ankles itch. And I nearly pull away while the sun kisses my graying head. Except that Scout, our tabby and white cat who is extremely elusive with her affections, stands near me, then weaves through my legs, purring, coursing in and out, head-butting my calves, looking up at me joyfully, then plopping herself in that pokey grass and rolling around for a heavenly scratch. She exhibits such bliss that the thought comes to me, *Why don't I love myself enough to do the things that make me happy?*

Scout doesn't care about the state of her feline waistline or the color of her fur. She simply lives happy in her skin and rolls and rolls and rolls with delight.

I start to believe in that moment, as the sun warms me, that God wants me to be like Scout. And he invites you to do the same.

Abandon yourself to joy.

Find what makes you happy and roll in it.

Wind in and through the footstool of the Almighty, purring, enraptured, alive.

It gives me great joy to see Scout have joy.

And it gives God great joy to see us have joy.

The problem is that we've believed the lie that only a certain body type or a particular age equals bliss.

I've bought into it. I've let culture, not Scripture, inform my worth in this area, to the point that it has so disabled me that I cannot even enjoy my life. Because I see myself as terribly flawed and unworthy, I don't take time to love myself or bless myself with practices that bring joy or exercise disciplines that might even enhance my beauty.

This cult of youth and beauty is a myth. But oh how we've believed it. We've devoured the lies, letting them sink into our marrow, forgetting that Jesus places a supreme value on our hearts. We've dismissed God's straightforward words to Samuel when he chose King David over his more attractive brothers: "Don't judge by his appearance or height, for I have rejected [Eliab]. The LORD doesn't see things the way you see them. People judge by outward appearance, but the LORD looks at the heart" (1 Sam. 16:7).

God looks at our hearts and values them.

We look at our bodies and devalue them, while our hearts emaciate.

There has to be a better way, a way of peace, where we embrace who we are and whose we are without abusing our bodies or shaming ourselves.

Being Honest about Body Image Struggles

First, let's define the heartache our appearance has wrought. I was once in a meeting where a woman, brave as an underdog in a fight for justice, raised her hand when attendees were asked to voice their prayer requests. "I have a prayer request," she said. You could hear the hesitation in her voice. Most requests revolved around health scares, wayward children, or financial worry. But hers stuck with me. "I can't seem to lose the last twenty pounds." Tears. "I've tried and tried, but I've hit a wall."

Women around the room nodded, knowing what she meant. Many of them also felt what she bravely shared.

I wanted to hug her in that moment because she was plain honest. She could have been you. She could have been me. We may not have the exact same struggle, but there is always something, an aspect of our appearance, we're ashamed of, so ashamed that we are seldom brave enough to acknowledge our feelings out loud.

Another woman once pointed to a nondescript mole on her arm. Honestly, I would never have noticed it. But she'd carried it around like an albatross. "I'm so embarrassed about it," she admitted.

You Empower What You Focus On

The word *focus* is powerful. When we focus on what we perceive is wrong with our appearance, we slip toward obsession. And when obsession has its way, it devours contentment. If, however, we ask God to see as he sees and focus on what is going on in our hearts, the part of us that will endure eternity, joy will choke out the discontentment. Maybe this is why Peter encouraged the women he knew by saying, "You should clothe yourselves instead with the beauty that comes from within, the unfading beauty of a gentle and quiet spirit, which is so precious to God" (1 Pet. 3:4). Remember that Peter wrote this as a married man. Perhaps he said this to his wife as a reminder that what is really valued in God's kingdom is inner beauty. We must focus on this truth—inner beauty—because obsessing about that is actually freeing.

Receive a Compliment and Find Joy

We know the truth about inner beauty. We preach about its merits to ourselves. But we don't believe inner beauty matters for much. We also do not believe it when others tell us of our outward beauty. Most of us have cheerleaders in our lives who tell us we're beautiful. But it's not enough. We dismiss their words, for whatever reason. We think, *Oh, they have to say that*. Here's the sad truth about me: I flat out do not believe my husband, Patrick, when he tells me, "You are beautiful."

I nod.

"You don't believe me, do you?" His eyes hold the kind of exasperation that comes from years of rejection of his compliments.

"I try to," I say. But do I? I have overvalued the proclamations our culture makes about beauty. In doing so, I have undervalued his genuine statements. I've come to realize that this is sin. It's me preferring the world over my husband. It's me believing a lie and disdaining the truth. And it hurts my husband. Deeply. The more I disbelieve his words, the more I place distance between us and injure his heart.

Patrick would agree with this statement: "There is nothing more rare, nor more beautiful, than a woman being unapologetically herself: comfortable in her perfect imperfection. To me, that is the true essence of beauty."[1]

Oh, to live this, to be comfortable in our own sagging skin. To be ourselves, joyfully so. To be filled with the Spirit instead of overflowing with insecurities.

Let's Redefine Beauty

I met Sue Keddy when we were speakers together in South Africa at a large women's conference. She was older than me, and her smile lit up the room. She told stories of God's unending faithfulness on the mission field when her young husband died. She scraped by and trusted God for provision—her faith was larger than the continent she served on. Her gorgeous, brave heart made me long to spend one hundred hours with her. When we parted after a week of getting to know each other, our hug was tearstained, and I felt like I'd lost a lifelong friend. Sue embodies beauty to me. Her eyes shine Jesus. Her arms embrace the broken. Her smile is a result of trusting God through extreme trials. Her body bears the marks of loving others. Her feet have run to the ends of the earth to see men and women set gloriously free. When she endured a car accident, her concern was for others. She prayed for the hospital staff. She lives counterintuitively for that beautiful, upside-down kingdom where the poor are rich, the marginalized are important, and the weak are boldly strong.

That is beauty.

But we have not defined it that way, have we?

As we take this journey toward wholeness, let's look at six truths that can catapult us toward believing our worth, particularly in the area of our appearance.

1. God Made Beautiful You

We know from Psalm 139 that God creates each one of us, knits us in our mama's womb, and declares us beautiful. I could spend sentences and paragraphs and pages trying to convince you of this, but I won't. It's the simple truth. God made you. He makes beautiful people. And because God created you, you are worthy.

2. You See True Beauty through the Kingdom of God

Our lives should not consist of morbid preoccupation with our declining bodies, faces, bones, skin. Instead, when we occupy ourselves with the kingdom of God, we become more open to seeing genuine, God-breathed beauty all around us. Columnist Lore Ferguson perfectly captures this paradox: "When I think back to the times I felt most beautiful, most nourished, most comfortable with my body and its natural curves and inclinations, they were not the times I was most in control of those things, but the times I worried least about them. They were the years when I worked hard at my vocation, invested deeply in the people in my life, cared little about the unruly nature of my hair and my crinkly eyes when I laughed large."[2] She found true beauty when she sought to see it in others, and what she saw had nothing to do with what our culture defines as perfected beauty. "Beauty wasn't about what was inside of me or even me myself. Beauty was all around me if I'd stop looking in the mirror long enough to see it. Beauty was in the people with gaps in their teeth and not in their thighs. Beauty was in people with wrinkles by the sides of their eyes, proof they'd laughed hard all their lives."[3]

3. When You Live for the World's Approval, You Miss True Beauty

At a women's conference I once attended, the weekend culminated in attendees writing something on a card and placing it below a wooden cross. You could write anything. Something you wanted to let go of. Give up. Turn away from. It took me a while to find the words. They flamed inside me, burning to get out. But putting them on the page like that, so stark and real, gave me pause. Would I dare let go of this?

What did I write? "My need for male attention."

Ouch.

But true.

It's been my companion these many years, this yearning to be seen as beautiful, desirable, pretty, attractive. As I walked my confession toward the large wooden cross looming before me, I prayed.

Dear Jesus, I want to be free of this. I'm tired of needing this. Please take it. Please help me be happy without it. I surrender. Oh, how I surrender. I want your filling to be enough. I'm tired of thirsting for empty things.

At the cross, I let go of the card, then picked up a preprinted verse of Scripture from the basket in front of me. I didn't read it until I got back to my seat. There, staring back at me, was the perfect answer to my embarrassing problem: "If you [really] love Me, you will keep *and* obey My commandments. And I will ask the Father, and He will give you another Helper (Comforter, Advocate, Intercessor—Counselor, Strengthener, Standby), to be with you forever" (John 14:15–16 AMP).

A realization: I'd been trying to fill an emotional hole with what I'd thought a father was supposed to give. I'd been groomed to believe that a father's love involved a predatory glance, the way I looked. But that is not pure love. That's a shaky, painful, empty substitute. I wrote this as I thought further about it: "I crave/craved the kind of attention I was groomed for. I believed that kind of love was what a true father's love was. I chased after what is bent on destroying me because that's what I thought (subconsciously) a father's love was. I had too low a view of genuine fatherly love. A distorted view. So I spent my life longing for something God didn't intend."

Scripture affirms a pure form of love: the constant comfort of the Holy Spirit. I sat thankful for the revelation—one I'd never thought of until that moment. I marveled at how beautifully the Lord unfolded it for me. And suddenly my "need" for male attention looked trivial. As C. S. Lewis once wrote, I satiated myself with mud pies when a holiday at sea beckoned. I want to be that Mary who chooses the good part, the God who won't be taken from her. I'm tired of filling myself with little gods, little subverted needs. And I'm ready for freedom, blessed freedom. Are you? Is this your struggle? Chasing men's compliments or whatever it takes to fill that void may work for a hesitant moment, but you'll always thirst for more. Quench your thirst instead in the audacious approval Jesus has for you right now.

4. Because God Made You, It's Honorable to Make Yourself a Priority

I battle self-discipline. There are weeks and months when I eat right, exercise, and take care of myself. I've participated in sprint triathlons and was even crazy enough to run a half marathon (I lived, but barely). I love to reminisce about these things. What I don't like to reflect on are all the in-between times that stretch longer and longer as the years go by, times when I eat Moose Tracks ice cream after 9:00 p.m. and skip my morning run in lieu of shut-eye in my comfortable bed. I am both as disciplined as an athlete in training and as undisciplined as my lazy, sleep-all-day cat.

And, oddly, on a recent run, I realized there was a connection between worth and discipline. When we exercise discipline in our lives, we are practicing a form of self-love. We see ourselves as valuable. We, fully assured of our place on this earth and our important role here (we are indispensable after all), take care of ourselves. We want to be about the kingdom of God, so we take care of our bodies and hearts and souls to maximize our impact.

Often this kind of healthy living springs from our feelings of worth. If we feel worthy of attention, worthy of health, worthy of kindness, then we will make the time to take care of ourselves, not feeling guilty about the effort but grateful for the opportunity.

Health is important to me on so many levels—physical, relational, spiritual, emotional, and mental. However, lately I've slipped quite a bit in the way I take care of myself. My friends remind me of this. Some are a bit alarmed at my pace of life. I tend toward workaholism, and I'm always so very tired. I am reactive about my health. If I am sick, I stop my life a bit and rest, hoping for recovery. But simply reacting won't produce lasting health. Great health comes from being proactive, from making incremental changes over the long haul. *Eat Move Sleep* by Tom Rath has helped cement this truth for me.

Small choices make for big change. I tend to be the big changes kind of person. I want to make monumental outward splashes. I forget that being faithful in small decisions actually changes life for the better, for the long haul. Jesus affirms this: "If you are faithful in little things, you will be faithful in large ones" (Luke 16:10).

Rath's book is about food, pace, and rest. We have the sweet (pun not intended) opportunity every day to make healthy food choices. We can control the pace of our lives in the way we take strategic breaks and exercise. Also, we must not forsake sleep for more productivity. He reminds us that stress is a killer. And how we live life in the little moments is how it will play out in the big moments.

As I thought about this and affirmed this truth, in true Mary style, I barged forward. I was going to be the best eater, exerciser, and sleeper known to man (and woman). This lasted 1.7 days. And then I was back to terrible choices, justifying lethargy and watching TV at night instead of slumbering. This is when I had mental breakdown #358. And I berated myself for being such a bad chooser. But then I stepped back and thought, *Self, why are you doing this? Why so much anger? Why is this hard for you?*

And, ultimately, it boiled down to the one thing God keeps bothering me about.

Worth. You may want a refund for this book now. Why would someone who struggles so much with worth write a book about it? Maybe it's so I can come alongside you as a friend, as a fellow worth-struggler. Maybe it's so I can let you know what's been helpful to me. Truth? Way deep down, I don't feel I'm worth taking time to take care of. I don't tend to value myself, so I can't sustain those small choices that lead to big change. I don't think I'm *worth* all the fuss.

So I've written this book asking God to help me see I'm worth it. And I'm asking the same for you. We are made in the image of an amazing, spectacular God who cherishes and adores us. He wants us to be kind to ourselves. Yes, yes, by all means make small choices that lead to big change. But do so with worth as your underlying motivation. Not to be cool. Not to be a "hottie." Not to foster bragging rights about your awesomeness. Do it simply because you are wildly loved by your Creator and worth taking care of.

5. Entropy Doesn't Have to Happen to Your Soul

Entropy, moving from order to disorder, attacks our bodies as we age. Health typically doesn't improve as we get older. Wrinkles happen. Sagging occurs. Weight piles on. Hairs gray. Eyesight wanes. Depressed yet? If this is true (and it is), then how do we live amid an appearance-driven culture that places high value on the youthful and little to none on graying people? The answer lies in a shift of perspective.

What God values is not what others value. He beautifies our insides, values our souls, our relationship with him and others. His mandate for discipleship doesn't decrease with age; it increases— meaning it's not how we begin our faith that ultimately matters but how we live out that faith with fear and trembling. Our goal is to grow closer to Jesus as we age so that while our bodies weaken, our souls grow stronger.

The greatest foe to soul beautification is bitterness. And this can take root in our depression stemming from how we look. We can become bitter about the aging process or that we aren't as pretty as other women or that we don't receive much attention anymore because we're not in our twenties. That's superficial bitterness. But what ushers in an ugly soul is the kind of bitterness that comes from unforgiveness. I've stepped into the puddle of unforgiveness only to find it a deep ocean of sadness, vengeful thoughts, and wrath that seems to have nowhere to go. And when I let it take root, I am not pretty.

I've watched people over the years—those who forgive and those who don't. And the gracious ones tend to have gracious souls. They're the kind of people you want to hang around with because they emulate Jesus's love. They're irresistible. Jesus, though he had no stately form according to Isaiah 53:2, was so attractive that crowds couldn't get enough of him. He, though unlovely, was irresistible. And that is what we, his followers, should be too.

Our inner radiance comes from this irresistibility. This love. This representation of the goodness of God. Every single woman on the face of this amazing earth has the potential to radiate God's outlandish beauty, despite her outward appearance. Every day we walk our journey is a day we step toward or away from that kind of beautification. When I hold my grandbabies someday, when my eyes grow dim, when I taste death, I want people to see beyond my fading physical body. I want them to look into my eyes and see irresistible Jesus shining there.

So entropy doesn't have to define our worth. The decline of our physical health and appearance doesn't mean our worth fades in like manner, although our culture would say otherwise, as it aggrandizes youth. We may even be young but in poor health. This, too, is not an indication of our worthlessness. Worth is settled in the person of Jesus Christ, and because the Spirit of God rests on and within us, we have the opportunity to grow a beautiful soul—one that shines brighter and more beautiful as years rage on. This is hope. This is power. This is countercultural. This is living in light of eternity, with an eye bent toward what God values.

The apostle Paul embraced this truth of a soul growing more beautiful with time. He writes, "That is why we never give up. Though our bodies are dying, our spirits are being renewed every day. For our present troubles are small and won't last very long. Yet they produce for us a glory that vastly outweighs them and will last forever! So we don't look at the troubles we can see now; rather, we fix our gaze on things that cannot be seen. For the things we see now will soon be gone, but the things we cannot see will last forever" (2 Cor. 4:16–18).

My sincere prayer is that this book starts a revolution of a renewed sense of worthiness for many people. And it's all because of the revelation of Jesus, who ultimately beautifies us all and deems us worthy of his love, despite how we feel about our appearance. I pray, too, that a day will come when we'll have the wild privilege of seeing one another not as the world sees us—through the lens of judgment, criticism, cynicism—but as God sees us—whole and good. Our new bodies will be a perfect reflection of the inner work he has done. In Paul's next breath, he discusses the paradox of our old and new bodies:

> For we know that when this earthly tent we live in is taken down (that is, when we die and leave this earthly body), we will have a house in heaven, an eternal body made for us by God himself and not by human hands. We grow weary in our present bodies, and we long to put on our heavenly bodies like new clothing. For we will put on heavenly bodies; we will not be spirits without bodies. While we live in these earthly bodies, we groan and sigh, but it's not that

we want to die and get rid of these bodies that clothe us. Rather, we want to put on our new bodies so that these dying bodies will be swallowed up by life. God himself has prepared us for this, and as a guarantee he has given us his Holy Spirit.

So we are always confident, even though we know that as long as we live in these bodies we are not at home with the Lord. For we live by believing and not by seeing. Yes, we are fully confident, and we would rather be away from these earthly bodies, for then we will be at home with the Lord. So whether we are here in this body or away from this body, our goal is to please him.

2 Corinthians 5:1–9

I love how Lore Ferguson comes to terms with this truth. She writes, "My body is not a tool to sharpen and shape, it is a tool for the ministry of the Holy Spirit. The feet that bring good news. The eyes that stare into the eyes of hurt people. The hands that minister healing. The body that curves itself to the brokenness it is surrounded by. God gave me this body, this life, and it is a vapor—passing away quickly, moment by moment."[4]

6. Focusing on Others' Beauty Changes the Way You View Your Own

She walked into the restaurant, and I felt in that moment she was stunning. Must've been about seventy years old, impeccably dressed, elegant, and just so very beautiful.

"Go tell her she's beautiful."

Really, Lord? I mean, I'm in this restaurant, and it's crowded, and people are all around. I don't know her. Don't you think that's a bit awkward?

I made a little bargain with God then. The woman sat across from a menu, obviously waiting for someone to show. If someone came and occupied the seat, I would officially be off the hook.

Funny the deals we strike with the Almighty. But no one came. Did I hear the laughter of God? The friend I had been dining with stood up to leave. I did too.

"I'll just be a second," I told her. "I need to do something really quick." So I walked over to the beautiful lady. "Excuse me," I said. "You don't know me, and I know this is kind of awkward, but I just felt like I needed to tell you that you are so beautiful."

She smiled. "What?"

"I felt you needed to know."

"Well, what is your name?" she asked.

"Mary."

She shook my hand and told me her name. "Thank you," she said. "But I'm so old. I don't have people telling me things like that."

"You are beautiful," I said.

"You are beautiful too," she said. "Inside and out."

I said good-bye and left the restaurant, so joyfully ecstatic that God had whispered such a simple thing to me and that I had chosen (after deliberation) to obey. I mean, how hard is it to tell someone she's beautiful? Perhaps we should spend our lives doing things like that, acknowledging one another's beauty.

I stand before a mirror, no longer feet to grass, and I look at myself. I am the heaviest I've ever been in the history of me, even pregnant me. That fact shames me. I look down. Scold myself. But then I remember my husband's words about how he thinks I'm prettier and prettier. I tell myself to focus on those words, to spend time concentrating on Patrick's truth, hoping it becomes my truth. I thank God for making me. I ask him to please help me be joyful in this skin he's given me. And then I sigh.

TRUTH:
God Made Beautiful Me.

Questions for Reflection or Discussion

1. How would a new acquaintance describe you? How do you feel about your body? What bothers you about it? What are you happy with?

2. You empower what you focus on. When have you obsessed over how you look? What was the result of that obsessing? When have you been happiest with your body? Why?

3. Is it easy or hard for you to receive a compliment? Why? Who in your life accepts compliments graciously?

4. In light of the Scripture passages in this chapter, how can redefining true beauty help you let go of worry about your beauty? What really matters in light of eternity? What does God value?

5. Write "God made me beautiful" on an index card and place it on your bathroom mirror. Dare to say that sentence out loud for a week. How does declaring this truth help you rethink the way you treat yourself?

6. When has someone told you about the beauty they found in you? Did you accept their compliment? Why or why not? When have you found beauty in someone else? How did she respond to your kind words?

7. How does making you a priority reflect self-worth? What roadblocks prevent you from being kind to yourself or choosing to be self-disciplined with food or exercise?

--- **WORTH PRAYER** ---

Jesus, I know you make beautiful people. It's easy for me to believe that about others but not about me. Help me view myself through your lens. Help me treat myself as kindly as I would treat my own daughter—by encouraging, speaking kindly to, and accepting myself. Help me focus on my inner beauty this week and see myself as a woman whose soul is gorgeous. And give me the unction I need to love myself enough to take care of myself. In the course of the next seven days, show me a beautiful woman I can compliment. Open my eyes to the beauty of others. Amen.

8

I Am Chosen

You did not choose Me but I chose you, and appointed you
that you would go and bear fruit, and that your fruit would
remain, so that whatever you ask of the Father in My name
He may give to you.

John 15:16 NASB

....

LIE:
I Deserve to Be Overlooked.
....

I long to be noticed, this is true. It's part of my DNA, and so often
God brings this up to me, this insatiable growl for recognition.
It manifests itself currently in my writing and speaking career, but
it has lurked inside me my entire life—I cannot remember a time
when I did not pine after being chosen.

I never made a sports team.

Never became a nominee for various courts in high school.

I became a vice president because I ran unopposed.

Never received a literary award. In fact, the one sweet recognition I did receive came because I worked so very hard—the Pacesetter Award, they called it. Not because of me but because of all the miles of words I produced.

I do truly appreciate what has come my way, but so much of it has been a result of grinding out productivity, outworking the others. Honestly, I'd rather just be picked because of me, not my output.

I know all the theological truths—I was chosen before the foundation of the world, God has prepared an amazing life for me if I simply walk in it, being picked in the kingdom looks entirely different from being picked by humans. But those humans and their fickle pickings defy my belief.

I met Amy while sitting at a round table during a meal at a conference. She was bright and faith-gutsy and the kind of person you want to have a three-hour conversation with. She came to the conference as a newbie, while I was a veteran. She was humble and wide-eyed. And she really didn't have expectations of the weekend. "I'm just so grateful to be here," she told me. She spoke of wild adventures she'd experienced around the globe as a nomad for Jesus—yes, she was that kind of awesome.

During our time at the conference, coaches evaluated our speaking skills. My coach picked me apart, even though the others in my group struggled to communicate but I did not. He heaped praise—great bouquets of encouragement—on them. I waited for a weed of praise but received none. I understood. I did. He figured I had thick-as-hide skin and would appreciate all the negative feedback.

But inside I cried. The girl who longed to be praised and picked shriveled, and I began to nurse a quiet distrust of my coach. At the end of the conference, I sat with Amy again. She shared all the praise she'd received from her coach, and then she said, "I really don't know what to say, but they've asked me to be a coach someday."

All my coach's negative words flooded my head, highlighting my unworthiness and undermining any confidence I had as a speaker. But these words to Amy hit me even harder. The powers that be had chosen the untested newbie over the years-of-practice veteran. *See*, the voices told me, *you are intrinsically unworthy of being picked. You are flawed in your being. No matter how well you perform, you will never merit attention. Besides that, you're past your prime. Don't you see how young and fun Amy is? How she lights up the people she is around? You don't light up others because you are far too busy hoping others will praise your light.*

That last sentence is true, and it is painful to admit in the pages of this book about worth. When we pine after being chosen, we forget that the entire world has the same deep need, and we cease from choosing them. So we all run around in circles hoping, hoping, hoping to be noticed, except that as we do that, we have no time or energy to dignify another person by picking them.

The thing was that I really liked Amy. So much. I wished her absolutely no harm and genuinely felt happy for her. I was glad she'd been chosen. But the problem came when I believed that someone else's success equaled my worthlessness. The two are unrelated, but I lived as if they were. Do you?

So on the way home from the conference, in the company of a new friend, I blubbered like a grieving woman. So many years of work, work, work, much of it wholly unobserved. The grief felt tangible, like a lurking monster pouncing on my resolve, siphoning off my perseverance. "It's not fair," I told her. "I'm so tired." I sucked in another breath while she sat quietly behind the steering wheel of the car, no doubt wondering if she was transporting an insane person.

All that work.

Unnoticed.

Unseen.

And as I said and cried those words, it dawned on me.

God saw.

He noticed.

He chose me.

And his plan was fully mysterious. It was hard to understand why some people get their big breaks without effort, while mule horses like me pound on the keyboard for years, still waiting for the one book to "hit."

This wasn't my time to be the It Girl.

It was my time to be the Sit Girl. The one who waits again. Anticipates the next. Trusts God's timing for success (or no success). Understands that his plan is a strange beast that never quite manifests the way we want it to but becomes clearer in retrospect.

It's been several years since I boohooed in anguish over not being chosen. Amy has no earthly idea her success undid me, and we have not crossed paths again. I'm a little more mature now, sporting a few more wrinkles (please let them be from smiling, not frowning!). I'm finding joy in unnoticed obedience. Way down deep, I understand it's part of God's mule-horse plan for me. Whether my books sell well or crash and burn, he has not revoked the work from me. I am to write still. As an act of worship. As an act of sheer, beautiful obedience.

And, honestly, I'm embarrassed. Because there is so much to be thankful for. In the great lineup of life, he has picked me because he ultimately gave his Son for me. In fact, he has picked all of us. Yet we wrongly believe that his picking is not enough to preserve our happiness. We think we will be fulfilled if or when those in authority (other than God) pick us, dignify us, herald us. We think, errantly, that people can fulfill our deepest longings for worth. This simply is not true.

Concentrate on Fruit

A synonym for chosen is picked. And when I think of the word *picked*, I think of picking fruit. One memory in particular flashes through my mind. I am younger than ten, and I'm climbing a cherry tree, the one that grows in and around our nearly dilapidated chicken coop. I climb higher and higher, more than ten feet off the ground, then probably twelve. I see a perfectly ripe cherry a few inches from my grasp. I scoot my body like an inchworm on the steady branch, though a bit of breeze makes it wag slightly. I swallow. Then I see the cherry again, redder than any of its friends. So I reach. Except that I cannot grasp it. I slide closer, extending my right arm toward the fruit. And then it happens. Air. Flailing arms. No branch. And certainly no cherry.

I fall with a thud to the ground, hitting my elbow, shattering my arm, dislocating my shoulder, and breaking various bones in the vicinity. I crawl my way to my mom, through the pasture, crying.

I was so intent on grabbing that fruit that I cared for nothing else, even when injury threatened.

The problem is that throughout life, we let go of picking—or concentrating on—fruit. We care more about being picked. Our lives become a stage on which we perform to garner the attention of the popular folks, all the while forgetting that we've already been picked by the Most Popular One.

Consider this famous passage where Jesus talks about picking:

> I no longer call you slaves, because a master doesn't confide in his slaves. Now you are my friends, since I have told you everything the Father told me. You didn't choose me. I chose you. I appointed you to go and produce lasting fruit, so that the Father will give you

whatever you ask for, using my name. This is my command: Love each other. If the world hates you, remember that it hated me first. The world would love you as one of its own if you belonged to it, but you are no longer part of the world. I chose you to come out of the world, so it hates you.

John 15:15–20

There are many truths we can pull from this dense piece of Scripture. First, of course, is that we didn't pick God; he picked us. We aren't excluded from the family of God. No longer slaves on the outskirts, we are welcomed by Jesus as friends, as chosen insider friends and family. For those of you who struggle with being chosen (I raise my hand high), this is amazing news. God has chosen us. Not only that, he beautifies and heals us. "He lifted me out of the pit of despair, out of the mud and the mire. He set my feet on solid ground and steadied me as I walked along" (Ps. 40:2).

Next, is this: we should not be preoccupied with being chosen by others. We've already settled that God, the Creator of all of the humans on this earth, has chosen us. Life should be consumed by producing great fruit. Just as the cherry tree I climbed created pie cherries for me to eat and pit and toss into pastry, God created us to do what should come naturally to us: bear fruit.

So be chosen by God. Bear fruit.

And what is that fruit?

Love. Other people. People just like you who desperately long to be chosen too. Part of your bearing fruit is choosing others to dignify and serve selflessly. By living this way, you are doing just what your Creator does every millisecond of every day: loving people.

And what will happen when you live this fruitful life of radical love? Some people will unpick you. They'll be mad because they're threatened by such selfless, loyal love. Why? Because it points to the kingdom of light. It hints at the beauty of God. It reflects a loving Creator. The kingdom of darkness does not like this at all.

It prefers favoritism, hierarchies, losers, alienation. When we live in the kingdom of darkness, we walk in these strange truths. James reminds us that this is sin.

> My dear brothers and sisters, how can you claim to have faith in our glorious Lord Jesus Christ if you favor some people over others? For example, suppose someone comes into your meeting dressed in fancy clothes and expensive jewelry, and another comes in who is poor and dressed in dirty clothes. If you give special attention and a good seat to the rich person, but you say to the poor one, "You can stand over there, or else sit on the floor"—well, doesn't this discrimination show that your judgments are guided by evil motives?
>
> James 2:1–4

These verses are about choosing according to the world's system, of preferring the strong over the weak, the rich more than the poor, the cool to the uncool. If you settle yourself into the truth that God has picked you and naturally accept others regardless of what they can do for you or your reputation, then you will live a life of worth. This leads to the next truth.

Choosing Others Lessens the Sting of Not Being Chosen

I have a friend who says she feels like an outcast. I know what she is referring to, as we both have woven in and out of trendy Christian women's circles, often feeling different, strange, alienated. Neither of us fits the mold, which unsettles us both. We found each other in the pain of exclusion and eased our wounds as we talked. Neither of us was alone. This experience has reminded me again just how many people feel left out in this world. And what a refreshing thing it is when we dare to choose those in that very familiar camp.

I have tried to follow the lead of one of my amazing friends who now dances with Jesus. If I could give her a title, it would be "The Grand Chooser" because she gravitated toward the lost, the lonely, and the hurting and dared to help each person, treating them as if they were the front man for U2 or the CEO of a gigantic company or a Hollywood star. She had love coursing through her veins, and although she no longer walks this earth, how she picked others reminds me to do the same.

I once chose one of her friends, who preferred to stay firmly out of the limelight, to help with a task I couldn't do that she was perfectly suited for. She was shy, reserved nearly to a fault, and she wanted to serve quietly without fanfare. To be honest, I deeply admired that about her. I wondered if she'd back away, but she accepted my tentative request with gusto. Now I have the supreme privilege of being her friend. She has a beautiful soul, yet many people overlook her. When I remember how insecure I am, how I long to be chosen, I think of this friend, and I smile. In choosing her, I suddenly have less need to be noticed. Isn't that how love works? That the more we love others, the less we worry about making people love and admire us? When we take our eyes off our constant neediness and focus instead on the needs of others, suddenly our needs shrink. We become more grateful. We remember that in giving to others, we actually give to ourselves. We are sowing that which we long for, and that changes us. We experience more of Jesus when we love his people than when we forcefully pine over being neglected.

Which leads to a caution.

You May Need to Protect Yourself from Worth Stealers

My heart sinks, to use a tired metaphor, but it's the correct wording because I can physically feel the lub-dup of its beat hollow out in my stomach. No. Not this. Not these accusing words—again. They weave in and out of my soul, shouting unworth. *You failed. You ruined. You bruised. You cannot be my friend unless you crawl back.*

Years before, this friend chose me. She went out of her way to sit me down and spill her friendship at my feet. And in the light of being picked like that, I began to diminish. You'd think I'd flourish, but instead I shrank. I, to my shame, valued the relationship more than I valued myself, my will, my essence. I didn't know it for years, but I had allowed another person's opinion to inform my worth. Shame seeped into me because I often felt unimportant in my friend's presence. I never pushed back, never asserted my views. I simply absorbed hers, and as long as I did, the friendship lived and moved and had its being.

However, the moment I pushed back, a rift deeper than the Columbia Gorge opened up. Some friendships exist well in a one-sided dynamic—one person right, the other wrong. They thrive in that settled arrangement. But when the wrong person grows weary of always being the broken one and wobbles on unsteady will and says, "I am allowed to have an opinion," either all hell breaks loose or the friendship evolves into something mutually beautiful.

This dynamic is an ancient one. I even experienced it with my husband a few years into our marriage. I told him, "You're perfect, and I'm yucky." Sometimes relationships work with one person being the designated mess and the other one pristine and perennially correct. Our most healing time came at Patrick's realization and confession that he had issues too. We walk side by side now, two broken people, and I don't shrink back in my unworthiness.

It's also happened to me in family relationships. I wonder if maybe I'm the common factor, the girl who prefers wearing the victim mask so the other person can feel better. As long as I wallow in my unworthiness, while they assert their rightness or perfection, we keep things as they are and never do the hard work to experience life as it could be—with honesty and humility and a dose of change for both. I've recently experienced a sweet thundering shift in a family relationship as well. Instead of having a relationship with one broken person plus one perfect person, we are rejoicing in a relationship founded on our mutual need for healing. It's a beautiful place.

And because of that beauty, the ache I feel right now overwhelms me. Unfortunately, my friend wants to stay in this painful, unequal dynamic. Last night as I drove, experiencing a brilliant Texas sunset, I made a hasty decision to just acquiesce, agree with her assessment, and save the relationship at any cost, even if it cost me my will. Capitulation would rule the day. I would agree with my awfulness and jump headlong back into the role I played but didn't like, where shame silenced my voice and I constantly felt like I'd never amount to anything.

I processed my sinking heart with Patrick, spilled out all the words about how I would just make things right by admitting to things I didn't even do. He steadied me. Told me the truth. Held my broken words in his open hands.

The conundrum looms before me. It's like I have to jump through hoops to be accepted, hoping that this is not how God's economy works.

Perhaps being chosen is so powerful because being rejected terrifies us.

Being rejected means we have no worth.

Being chosen means we have it all.

So we contort ourselves in whatever impossible positions we can to make ourselves chooseable. We let go of our will, conform our lives to make others approve, and lose our personalities at the altar of being picked.

Maybe you have a relationship that constantly undermines your worth. I won't write a pat answer about how to deal with "worth stealers" because all relationships are different, and some can't simply be disregarded. But I will encourage this: pray. Ask God to open your eyes to the people in your life who bring you down. Many terrific books are available to help you establish boundaries around yourself for protection. Relationships are messy things. But perhaps your worth is not being settled today because you believe and value a bully's loud opinion of you over the still, small voice of the God who adores you.

Don't Become Someone Else Just So You'll Be Chosen

A lot of pain and insecurity come from masks we wear. We don them because we perceive someone (or a group of someones) won't like us unless we look exactly like them or do the things they deem acceptable. When we do gain acceptance, insecurity mounts. We ask ourselves, *If they only know the me who puts on an act, will they love the real me?* Some folks go through identity crisis after identity crisis because they've become adept at life as a chameleon—saying or doing or becoming what others want instead of actually embracing who they are.

Thankfully, God already knows every secret, every act, every mask. He knows the real us and loves us. If we can internalize that truth, then we'll be more apt to be perfectly ourselves, not worrying whether people like or embrace us. We'll live with the secret joy of knowing our Creator adores us, picks us, wants us, even if others reject us.

The Pharisees were a group of religious leaders who perfected the art of wearing masks. Not only that, but they forced these perfection masks onto others. So everyone walked around pretending to be awesome, conforming to everyone else's expectations. They even added to God's expectations, saddling folks with deeper, wider, stronger regulations—heavy yokes that no human was designed to bear. I wonder, as I consider the Pharisees, just how insecure each one was. Did they look at their reflections in the Sea of Galilee and shudder? Did they bicker and fight to be picked? I'm guessing yes.

But Jesus shattered all their carefully constructed masks. He messed with the boundaries, the limits, the rules. He brought every human being down to the essential level—ignoring the fluff, the preening, the special clothes, the right rituals—and looked at only one thing: the heart. All of us fail the heart test. No mask can cover up a sinful heart under the heated gaze of the Almighty. We all fall short.

So why try to fight for recognition? Why be someone else when it doesn't really matter? Jesus loves every bit of us. He loves our hearts. He wants us to be real—ourselves, utterly honest. He empowers us as we are. And he values the variety of the human race. Jewish literature reinforces this truth. "Our Rabbis taught: [The creation of the first man alone] was to show forth the greatness of the Supreme King of kings, the Holy One, blessed be He. For if a man mints many coins from one mould, they are all alike, but the Holy One, blessed be He, fashioned all men in the mould of the first man, and not one resembles the other."[1]

Conformity runs contrary to the King of kings. Variety better expresses him because he cannot be fully explored or fathomed, and each of us bears a unique taste of his goodness (which is why we all have our different shapes, wants, backgrounds, gifts). Instead of categorizing people into who is chosen based on culture's valued traits, let's remember that God chooses foolish people first—the broken, the needy (1 Cor. 1:26–29). God's penchant for choosing anyone and everyone, no matter their traits, eliminates the need for wearing a mask, doesn't it?

David, the shepherd boy, knew himself and trusted God. Although David was often overlooked as the runt of the litter, his quiet obedience in the pastures merited closeness to God. Think about it. He only had himself, God, and sheep. No one else to turn to. No one else to impress. Just happy bleating and the silence that comes from barren wilderness. In that crucible of aloneness, he learned he didn't need a mask to impress God, didn't need to be anyone but himself. Which is what we learn when we walk through our own wildernesses. The wilderness purifies us down to the elements: us, God, and the circle of relationships he entrusts to us.

David remained true to himself, settled into his worth. He was chosen first by God in the sheep fields, then by Saul to fight the scary giant Goliath on the battlefield. Saul worried about David and his brash confidence, so he offered the shepherd boy his armor. The problem was that the armor, fit for tall King Saul, hung off David's body and hindered him. He clanked around awkwardly as the giant shouted insults. No, David had to shed Saul's armor to fight the fight before him. He had to be himself, relying fully on God's bigness and protection. David asserted, "This very day the LORD will deliver you into my hand! I will strike you down and cut off your head. This day I will give the corpses of the Philistine army to the birds of the sky and the wild animals of the land. Then all the land will realize that Israel has a God and all this assembly will know that it is not by sword or spear that the LORD saves! For the battle is the LORD's, and he will deliver you into our hand" (1 Sam. 17:46–47 NET).

The truth? Be you. Be blessedly, awkwardly, totally you. Don't become someone else in order to be chosen. And once you are chosen, don't try to wear battle armor tailored to someone else. Remember, God is your deliverer. He wants you to love this world in your own you-shaped way. He isn't calling you to be her or that speaker or that woman. He is calling you to be unashamedly you. If only you would grasp this wildly beautiful acceptance of you unplugged, you being all you. It's time to stop cowering to the demands of others, including well-meaning Christians who try to define what a Christian woman should or shouldn't be, whose armor she should wear, and how she should talk.

God's church isn't a robot army of identical warriors. It's a body of mismatched, unpicked (but picked) pilgrims who dare to live unmasked. It's people slowly becoming more and more and more of themselves.

God has chosen you. All your quirks. All that baggage. All those secret and not-so-secret failures.

You.

Are.

Chosen.

Now run, oh chosen one, run.

....

TRUTH:

God Has Chosen Me.

....

Questions for Reflection or Discussion

1. What memory stands out to you regarding getting picked or being overlooked? How has that memory affected you today?

2. How does concentrating on the fruit you can produce lessen the need to be picked by others?

3. Who in your life loves to pick people? What have you learned from them?

4. When has choosing others helped you get over feeling left out? What happened?

5. Who are the worth stealers in your life? How can you navigate around them? What has God specifically been saying to you about them in this chapter?

6. When have you wanted to become someone else or conform to something you're not in order to be picked or noticed? How did you feel afterward?

7. Do you feel the church culture you're currently involved in has cliques? Why or why not? What can believers do to ensure more people get picked?

───────── WORTH PRAYER ─────────

Jesus, when I don't get picked, I panic. I feel small and worthless. Instead of letting me stay in that painful place, will you alert me to those who feel the same way? Please help me become a picker of people. Give me discernment in dealing with the worth stealers who come my way. Help me set appropriate boundaries and still practice your unconditional love. I want to be solely me, not conforming to what everyone expects of me just to fit in. Enable me to be the most gracious me I can become, one who seeks those who feel left out. Amen.

9

I Am Destined for Impact

As I have said, the first thing is to be honest with yourself. You can never have an impact on society if you have not changed yourself. . . . Great peacemakers are all people of integrity, of honesty, but humility.

Nelson Mandela

LIE:
My Life Makes Zero Impact.

You would not have known by looking at my friend Mike that he had once walked as a giant on this earth. His once pink, healthy skin had become a sallow color due to liver failure. With yellowing eyes and a hesitant gait, he happened into our lives in the oddest sort of way, which is also how Jesus happens into our lives—unexpectedly.

149

By happenstance, Patrick became a Sunday school teacher a few weeks after he'd been asked to simply join a class. The teacher pulled him aside and said, "I am leaving. Can you teach it?" We inherited the class then. It was a group of crazy awesome folks, people who either had recently met Jesus after hard living or had been church-burned and were making tentative steps back into the scariness of fellowship. Mike walked into that room and immediately and humbly captured our hearts.

He'd lived a prodigal life, finding rock bottom too many times to count, until he literally faced death from disease, met Jesus, and started living on this earth with shiny eyes. Today, as I'm bothered by celebrity pastors wearing bling, having handlers, and living in multimillion-dollar compounds, I think of Mike's simplicity. How this frail man, nearing death, would go out of his way to help others.

When a friend of ours was dying from a brain tumor, Mike and our Sunday school class volunteered to clean up his family's yard, which had been neglected during the man's illness. Mike could barely walk, and his skin seemed yellower under the pale winter sun. He could do very little physical work without exhausting himself, but he persevered. He sat on the front cement porch under the yawning two-story entrance and dug with a hand shovel uniform holes in the earth into which he placed tulip bulbs. He carefully covered each promise of spring with dirt. The way he smoothed the soil over those bulbs you'd think he was gently putting grandchildren to bed.

The man with the tumor breathed his last. And in the spring those bulbs birthed brilliant, but a month later, Mike also lost his battle against death on a cold operating table. Mike self-published a book called *The Secret* about his conversion. I read his story when I began my career as a writer. His grammar is rough and his spelling is a mess, but that book is still one of my most prized possessions.

Jesus reminded me clearly of this truth the next time I sat down at my computer to write: "When you write," he impressed on me, "remember Mike." Because that dear, dear man was so much like Jesus. He was beautifully humble and sweetly kind, and he truly emanated the risen Christ. However, no one would choose him from a lineup of Christian celebrities. He'd be just like David, who was shepherding his flocks in obscurity when Samuel was tasked to pick the next king. Samuel had to beg the boy's father to bring all his sons to him, even the one who was left out. And that's who Mike was to me. Small in the world's sight, perhaps, but a man after God's heart—a giant of the faith in God's economy.

All that to say, take heart you who read these words and wonder if your life will ever amount to something flashy. Those who have had the deepest influences on my faith have been people whom the world overlooks. A man from India who exudes Jesus. A neighborhood woman who loves to do unnoticed things, hates fanfare, and adores behind-the-scenes encouragement. A poverty-touched man in Ghana who unfolds his story of faith before me; it is so beautiful that it feels like a lavish gift. A man and woman in Mexico who have quietly spent their lives caring for those less fortunate and have taken in a young boy because God told them to. A radio host from Iraq whom I won't meet until heaven's shores who suffered for years in prison because he loved Jesus relentlessly and without pomp or admirers. A woman in Kuala Lumpur who worships Jesus like no one I've ever seen—abandoned, committed, in love. A friend in Texas who spends herself on her knees where no one sees her toiling in prayer for many, many people. A Canadian woman who dares to find joy as a widow and hears from Jesus in personal, poignant ways. These people are in my hall of faith. They have no acclaim, no platform, no audience, but they join my friend Mike as some of the most profound examples of Jesus I have ever encountered.

Fame doesn't ensure impact. Often it degrades the very life of simple, Jesus-pursuing faith. The absolute perfect beauty of God's kingdom is that the big will be demoted and the meek promoted. So when you see others with gigantic ministries and you're tempted to despair that you will have so little impact in comparison, *rejoice*. Rejoice because our God rewards those who love him in the small places, who serve him in obscurity and secret.

Your worth before a holy God has absolutely nothing to do with numbers or crowds or ministries. Your worth is dignified because he loves you—simple as that. Thankfully, his measuring stick is different from the world's. You are worthy because you're loved, just like Mike was loved and had no earthly idea how many people walked into the kingdom because of his witness. In his book, he wrote, "I wake up every morning happy to be alive. Life is indeed what we make it. We just have to trust in God and believe there are things we will not know or understand. We should do the best we can to reach out to other people in need."[1]

We are all destined for impact, because we are loved by the Father and transformed by his radical grace. But how do we find our work in this world? And how do we determine what God has uniquely gifted us to do?

Go to the Movies

I can't remember when I first heard about this exercise, but I've been sharing it with people ever since. It helps you find your purpose, your reason for being on this earth, because it empowers you to see how you are unique. Grab a piece of paper, and without much deep thought, write down your three favorite movies. They can be as eclectic as you like. For instance, mine are *To Kill a Mockingbird*, *Return of the Jedi*, and *Strictly Ballroom* (an indie film made in Australia).

Now find the thread that weaves through all three of your favorite movies. For instance, in my three, outcasts become brave to resolve an injustice. The theme you find in your picks hints at your purpose. It's a little spooky, but it makes sense. Movies get at the deeper part of us, and pinpointing the stories that influence us helps us see what we might not normally see.

Am I an outcast who becomes brave to resolve injustice? Yes, though there are days the bravery eludes me.

Find the Intersection

Frederick Buechner wrote, "The place God calls you to is the place where your deep gladness and the world's deep hunger meet."[2] When I ask a room full of people what they perceive is the world's deepest hunger, it's surprising how many different answers I receive. You would think the answer would be unanimous, like "The world's deepest hunger is Jesus." But simply answering that question hints at your unique take on the world, based on how you've lived and the wisdom God has brought your way through trials and triumphs. My answer? The world's deepest hunger is to be healed from past pain.

Next, look at what your deepest gladness is. I liken this to your unique talents and passions. In other words, if I were to take a cross section of a hundred thousand people, then look at you, how would you differ from them? What makes you utterly stand out? What are you uniquely gifted to do? Sing? Build skyscrapers? Encourage others? Quietly serve? My deepest gladness, and what makes me stand out from others, is communication. I am gifted at writing and speaking about God's truth in an authentic way.

The sweet spot, where you'll experience the most joy and impact, is the intersection of those two. When you operate in this realm, you tap into the why—the purpose—of your existence. I believe I was placed on this earth not merely to live, breathe, then die but to communicate how people can be set free from the pain in their lives. That's what makes me sing. That's what makes me get out of bed in the morning.

So write down the world's deepest hunger and your unique gladness. Intersect them. If at least some of your life is spent in that specific pursuit, joy will come as you partner with Jesus to accomplish what only you can accomplish on this earth.

Be Prunable

Recently, I dug in the dirt and cleaned up the yard, listening to the birds chirp as I messed myself with soil and worms and plants. And then I pruned back deadwood on several plants and trees. I realized something quite startling as I cut spent branches: the dead ones were easier to snap than the live ones. Brown deadwood is easier to prune than green, living wood. And when you prune back the deadwood, the live wood has the best chance to flourish. In that moment, I remembered Jesus's words in John 15 about pruning, how the Father prunes back our branches so we'll yield more fruit. *What if*, I thought, *we would rather have the deadwood and not let it be pruned? What if we envisioned our ministry lives as doing A, when God wanted to cut back A so B would grow? To prune the dead in favor of the living?*

(And what if I didn't like that?)

Then the deeper questions came: *What if what I want isn't what God wants? What if I have been coddling dying branches in hopes of doing something significant? What if the real work God has for me has been trying to grow, but I've been neglecting it because I've clung to the deadwood?*

Perhaps an example will help.

Let's say Angie's life has been utterly changed by a speaker who spoke amazing God-breathed words. Angie thinks, *I want to do what that speaker does. I want other people to be changed just like I was changed.* So Angie works for years to build a speaking career, pursuing it at the cost of other ministries, because she believes speaking is what God wants her to do. Then one day she realizes God has wired her not to speak to thousands but to share life one-on-one as a mentor to troubled girls.

What she wanted: to impact the world, one stage at a time.

What God possibly intended: to impact the world, one person at a time.

Currently, I'm asking these tough questions. I wonder if what I want and what God wants are the same things. I question if perhaps my dreams are deadwood in need of pruning so the green wood will grow. I'm curious where the next pruning will happen—and how painful it will be.

Ever been in that place? You worked on what you thought was the next big thing only to realize that maybe it wasn't the pursuit God had planned for you.

I am in the process of pruning. But here's what I want: I want to follow the path God has for me. I want to be meek enough to realize when I'm trying to produce ministry on deadwood. I want to walk in the footsteps God has laid before me instead of trying to force him to follow my plan. God's plan must prevail. And I must be still and quiet enough to know when I'm getting in the way.

Embrace Focus

I'm an artsy person, with ideas ping-ponging in my brain at a scary tempo. And every idea seems to carry the same weight, which makes for a frenetic and burned-out Mary. But in order to truly help others, I need to focus on a few small things. I need to concentrate on providing high value. Which means no more burned-out Mary! I am learning to let go of the good and kind-of-okay for the sake of focusing on the great things I can do to bring better clarity and healing. I am asking the Spirit to guide me every single day so I don't run around reacting to life. Instead, I obey the still, small voice of God. Unfortunately, I have been more reactionary Mary than intentional Mary. So the learning to focus helps.

I recently listened to a fascinating exchange on National Public Radio about the productivity of researchers after they receive a prestigious award. It turns out that those who win academic awards early in their careers are the least productive later. Why? Because they branch out from their very narrow focus and try their hands at other things. Great success comes not from doing many things well (what a lie!) but from doing one thing with amazing genius.[3]

This is the power of focus, of concentrating on narrow tasks rather than becoming a jill-of-all-trades. I've found the more I focus, the greater joy I have when I complete one project. And that joy helps me understand and experience my worth. God hasn't called us to do everything pretty well. He's called us to do a few things very well.

Realize That Not All Gifts Are for Public Benefit

As you examine your unique gifts, you may realize that some gifts are not meant for public consumption but were given to you for your healing. I've seen this operate in my life as a writer. Some of my least successful books actually were the greatest tools God used to further me along my healing journey.

At one time, I believed God had placed me on this earth to lead worship. But I learned something after I sat in my small French living room pounding on my poor guitar, desperately trying to lead worship. I had a heart to worship and a voice that worked fine. I'd sung in contests and choirs and on worship teams. I loved Jesus. But when I had to lead worship songs in French, my brain pretty much exploded as I tried to remember chords and Jesusy French words.

And then I met Grace, the daughter of my friend Jeanne. This girl had talent. Playing with her in the room humbled bad-guitar-playing me, particularly when I heard her strum and sing. Performing is what she is meant to do. Grace is now part of First Aid Arts, a group of counselors, artists, and other people who work to bring healing to people through the arts.

I thought back to my times of wanting, wanting, wanting to be a worship leader. How I made a gutsy declaration to a small congregation (and freaked them out). How I tried out for the worship team at my big ol' church, only to fail the audition.

I was good. But I wasn't great.

So why all this need to worship?

I believe this gift is meant for my sake—not for the audience of others. It's so the Audience of One can heal me. When life has thrown lemons, worship has been my lemonade. Singing my way out of darkness has happened uncountable times. And I'm grateful for it. I am not meant to sing for crowds. I am meant to sing for me, for Jesus. It's okay. God gives us some gifts simply to heal us, not to proclaim them to the world.

Maintain an Eternal Perspective

My editor friend Sarah has stumbled onto something important pertaining to work: find an eternal perspective in what you do, keeping the extremely long view in mind. She writes:

> My short journal entry was self-talk on the difference between writing for the temporal and writing for the eternal. What perspective do I have when I write? Where is my heart focused when the

message takes form and the words flow out? But then I saw a line I had written that stopped me. "What are the pressures that make writing difficult?" To which I answered, "A sense of worthlessness." Writing with an eternal perspective is about obedience and knowing that the results are his. It's about dying to myself—dying to my desire to be known in public and my desire to stay hidden. Hiding means there is fear of something; dying to that fear enables, through the power of the Holy Spirit, the things that actually matter to be shared. Fear paralyzes. Writing with an eternal perspective is about dying to fear, about dying to my sense of worthlessness. It's about giving hope.[4]

Hope is wrapped up in our view of eternity, of how we see our lives playing out not on a temporal stage but on an everlasting one. Eternity informs our worth and work because what we do is remembered. Everything is cataloged, even the unseen things. God sees it all: "Now if any man builds on the foundation with gold, silver, precious stones, wood, hay, straw, each man's work will become evident; for the day will show it because it is to be revealed with fire, and the fire itself will test the quality of each man's work. If any man's work which he has built on it remains, he will receive a reward. If any man's work is burned up, he will suffer loss; but he himself will be saved, yet so as through fire" (1 Cor. 3:12–15 NASB). That word *remain* engenders hope, doesn't it? Nothing is wasted. No act is forgotten. This jives with the way Jesus encouraged us to see the kingdom of God—the last become first, the unnoticed find holy applause, the overlooked are seen.

This life is incredibly short, and we have only the moment in front of us to hear God and make a difference. We must ask God to "teach us to number our days, that we may gain a heart of wisdom" (Ps. 90:12 NIV). Paul reminds us of life's brevity and our responsibility to live it well: "So be careful how you live. Don't live like fools, but like those who are wise. Make the most of every opportunity in these evil days. Don't act thoughtlessly, but understand what the Lord wants you to do" (Eph. 5:15–17).

Randy Alcorn tells us to live in light of that final day of our lives, when our breath stops and we wake up on heaven's shores. "Heaven marks the beginning of an eternal adventure, but the end of earth's window of opportunity. One moment after we die, we will know exactly how we should have lived. But there will be no more second chances. As there will be no opportunity for the unbeliever to go back to earth and live his life again and this time to put faith in Christ, so there will be no opportunity for the believer to go back and relive his life, this time for Christ."[5]

May it be that we live in light of our worth, impacting our world as we contemplate eternity.

Be Generous

It's important to live a generous life. People are simply happier when they have the long view in mind and serve others rather than demand to be served. Jesus said, "For even the Son of Man came not to be served but to serve others and to give his life as a ransom for many" (Mark 10:45). Martin Luther King Jr. said, "Every man must decide whether he will walk in the light of creative altruism or in the darkness of destructive selfishness."

Author Adam Grant, in his groundbreaking leadership book *Give and Take*, does an incredible job of telling compelling stories of amazing givers, while surprising the reader and providing data. One of the most important things I took away from the book was how to be what he calls "otherish." He writes that those who are otherish "take care about benefiting others, but they also have ambitious goals for advancing their own interests."[6] So it's terrific to be a giver, but not a burned-out giver who constantly says yes to everything.

Successful givers don't overgive without heeding their own needs. They've learned to do what Jesus commanded—love others *as* we love ourselves. Givers who live without boundaries and spend life being taken advantage of eventually fail. But givers who learn to set boundaries and love themselves (in a non-self-absorbed way) succeed.

Grant shared some of his insights on my blog. He wrote, "My favorite feature of giver success is that it lifts others up, rather than cutting others down. When givers achieve excellence, they do so in ways that enable others to succeed as well, sharing credit, connections, and expertise. For givers, it's also less lonely at the top: we reserve the greatest admiration and respect for successful people who are generous. A third intriguing pattern is that people support successful givers, rather than gunning for them."[7] This sounds a lot like blessing others, loving them as Jesus does, and loving ourselves enough to take care of our schedules and hearts. In other words, we learn to become generous with others at the same time we are generous with ourselves. A person with high worth values both.

You are destined to make an impact on this broken world. God has uniquely shaped you to go places no one else will ever go, to love people in your circle whom even the president of the United States or Taylor Swift or a Nobel Peace Prize winner could not. Living in light of your gifts and strengths, even embracing them, will reinforce your worth. Not that your work defines you, but that you redefine the world through your work.

TRUTH:

The World Needs My Unique Contribution.

Questions for Reflection or Discussion

1. Who has had the greatest impact on your walk with Jesus? Why?

2. What three movies came to mind while you read this chapter? What is the thread that weaves through all three? Does that thread hint at your unique passion?

3. What is the world's deepest hunger? What is your unique gladness? How do they intersect?

4. In examining your life right now, what is the deadwood that needs to be pruned away? When have you superimposed your will onto God's in the area of ministry and purpose? (Or have you?)

5. How would your next year change if you chose to focus on one ministry?

6. When has a spiritual gift you've loved become a private way for God to heal you? Has God ever stripped away a public gift in order to bless you privately? In what ways has God chosen to heal you?

7. How does having an eternal perspective (seeing things in light of heaven) help you redefine your purpose?

─────────── WORTH PRAYER ───────────

Jesus, I want to impact this world, but in the best me-shaped way possible—in the way you have designed me. Help me unearth my passions and clearly see how they intersect with the needs of this world. Forgive me for wanting my ministry to be one thing when you may want it to be another. Prune me however you see fit. Use whatever gifts you've given me to help me heal from the past. And most important, help me keep the long view in mind, living life in light of hereafter, choosing to glorify you above all. I want to see you smile over my life. Amen.

10

I Am Worth More
than a Paycheck

That is why I tell you not to worry about everyday life—
whether you have enough food and drink, or enough clothes
to wear. Isn't life more than food, and your body more than
clothing? Look at the birds. They don't plant or harvest or
store food in barns, for your heavenly Father feeds them. And
aren't you far more valuable to him than they are?

Matthew 6:25–26

....

LIE:
My Worth Is Tied
to the Bottom Line.

....

I understand the upside-down kingdom—that those who are
first will be last and that money is a poor indication of our

state before God and doesn't necessarily equal favor. However, we in the United States have let the cultural myth of prosperity inform our worth.

This whole notion is really quite silly considering many Christians struggle to survive and battle poverty yet are rich in faith. I know better. I remember my friends in Ghana and how they first run to Jesus because money cannot rescue them as it seemingly does in the States. Their faith grows in deprivation, but we for some reason feel our faith should make us prosper.

Like Job, I discern the futile dynamics of wealth, that God gives and takes away, and we are to bless his name in either state. When we lost our home to fraud and foreclosure, although it took me a long time to get there, I found deep freedom in praising God despite our economic uncertainty. I'm well versed in proverbs like this one: "Do not toil to acquire wealth; be discerning enough to desist. When your eyes light on it, it is gone, for suddenly it sprouts wings, flying like an eagle toward heaven" (Prov. 23:4–5 ESV).

The New Testament Greek word for "worthy" is *axios*. It means weighing, having weight, having the weight of another thing of like value, worth as much, befitting, congruous, corresponding to a thing, of one who has merited anything worthy (in both a good and a bad sense).[1] We find it in this verse (among others): "Yet there are some in the church in Sardis who have not soiled their clothes with evil. They will walk with me in white, for they are worthy" (Rev. 3:4). And two chapters later:

> And I saw a strong angel, who shouted with a loud voice: "Who is worthy to break the seals on this scroll and open it?" But no one in heaven or on earth or under the earth was able to open the scroll and read it.
>
> Then I began to weep bitterly because no one was found worthy to open the scroll and read it. But one of the twenty-four elders

said to me, "Stop weeping! Look, the Lion of the tribe of Judah, the heir to David's throne, has won the victory. He is worthy to open the scroll and break its seven seals."

Then I saw a Lamb that looked as if it had been slaughtered, but it was now standing between the throne and the four living beings and among the twenty-four elders. He had seven horns and seven eyes, which represent the sevenfold Spirit of God that is sent out into every part of the earth. He stepped forward and took the scroll from the right hand of the one sitting on the throne. And when he took the scroll, the four living beings and the twenty-four elders fell down before the Lamb. Each one had a harp, and they held gold bowls filled with incense, which are the prayers of God's people! And they sang a new song with these words:

> "You are worthy to take the scroll
> and break its seals and open it.
> For you were slaughtered, and your blood has ransomed
> people for God
> from every tribe and language and people and nation.
> And you have caused them to become
> a Kingdom of priests for our God.
> And they will reign on the earth."

Then I looked again, and I heard the voices of thousands and millions of angels around the throne and of the living beings and the elders. And they sang in a mighty chorus:

> "Worthy is the Lamb who was slaughtered—
> to receive power and riches
> and wisdom and strength
> and honor and glory and blessing."

Revelation 5:2–12

Worth means weight, value, a precious commodity. It's a banking term. Yet in the Revelation passage, we see what God views as ultimate worth: Jesus Christ. To find our worth, we must first run to the Worthy One, the One equipped to settle our worth once and for all, for now and for eternity.

The math is simple: Jesus is worthy. He made us. He sacrificed his life for us. He rose again for us. Therefore, we are worthy.

But we forget our worth. We might know Jesus has great value, but who are we in light of his perfection? We recite verses about our value, yet they fall on deaf hearts. "Who can find a virtuous woman? for her price is far above rubies" (Prov. 31:10 KJV). The Hebrew word translated "virtuous" is *mekker*, which means value.

Except that when we experience difficult financial times or struggle to make ends meet, we feel defeated and worthless. Even though I know better, I still measure my worth by the bottom line. Not that I want to be rich (and I fully understand that living where I do in the house we have connotes wild wealth compared to many people), but somehow I believe that commensurate pay for what I do will make me fully satisfied. If I am paid what I am "worth," I will finally feel worthy.

As a writer, I've struggled for a decade to make putting words on the page a nominally compensated career. There have been many times when I have come to the brink of giving up and throwing ultimatums heaven's way, only to be rescued by God in the ninth hour. I do know that he has called me to this crazy business. I know this like I discern the freckles on my arms. I'm intimately acquainted with the stories of God's direction, whispers, and faithfulness. However, when it comes right down to it, I feel worthless because I cannot make what I should to help our family. I know I'm not alone in this. I've had enough near-successes to keep me bound in a frustrating cycle. And there are times when I wonder if God is thwarting my success because I need the discipline. Or because he wants to keep me humble.

When I've shared this with more successful friends, often I heard this back: "Of course God wouldn't thwart you. That's not what he does. He brings success." Really? When I think about the monetary state of the twelve disciples or the poverty of Jesus (rightfully the most successful man of all time in terms of eternal impact), I cannot abide by this strange thinking.

Paul learned the secret of true success when he penned, "I know how to live on almost nothing or with everything. I have learned the secret of living in every situation, whether it is with a full stomach or empty, with plenty or little" (Phil. 4:12). Financial success has nothing to do with our ultimate success. What does define us is our ability to be content no matter what happens to us.

I read quotes like this from author Adam Grant and try to remember that making a difference in other people's lives is more important than financial remuneration: "When people know how their work makes a difference, they feel energized to contribute more."[2] The key for me is to learn that the feedback I receive about my words and work is valuable and should have greater weight in my mind. For example, I recently received a letter from a woman who had read one of my books. In it she explained how much the book had helped her. True success is making a difference in the life of one survivor who is healing.

Unfortunately, our world revolves around prosperity. Money represents freedom and control. If we have it, we tend to feel free and in control. But if we lack it, we often feel helpless and shackled to need. We may be tempted to become prideful if we are financially successful. Or we may despair of our worth if we aren't.

The Bible warns us about the lure of wealth, its seduction.

> But that is the time to be careful! Beware that in your plenty you do not forget the LORD your God and disobey his commands, regulations, and decrees that I am giving you today. For when you have become full and prosperous and have built fine homes to live in, and when your flocks and herds have become very large and your silver and gold have multiplied along with everything else, be

careful! Do not become proud at that time and forget the LORD your God, who rescued you from slavery in the land of Egypt. Do not forget that he led you through the great and terrifying wilderness with its poisonous snakes and scorpions, where it was so hot and dry. He gave you water from the rock! He fed you with manna in the wilderness, a food unknown to your ancestors. He did this to humble you and test you for your own good. He did all this so you would never say to yourself, "I have achieved this wealth with my own strength and energy." Remember the LORD your God. He is the one who gives you power to be successful, in order to fulfill the covenant he confirmed to your ancestors with an oath.

Deuteronomy 8:11–18

The New Testament also warns of the lure of riches: "People who long to be rich fall into temptation and are trapped by many foolish and harmful desires that plunge them into ruin and destruction" (1 Tim. 6:9).

Yet we still persist in thinking if we had all the money we needed (wanted), we would finally be happy. You may remember the scene from the popular movie *It's a Wonderful Life* where George Bailey is chatting with his assigned angel, Clarence, about financial stress. Clarence asks George to let him help. George asks him if he happens to have $8,000 on him. Clarence tells George that money isn't used in heaven, to which George says, "Well, it comes in real handy down here, bud!"

Money sure does come in handy down here. It solves problems. Helps us quit worrying. And sometimes validates our existence. How can we find our worth in light of how God views it? Seven ways.

1. God Will Provide

"I'm agonizing over this," a dear missionary friend told me over the phone. "We really need a break, just a few days, but I'm struggling with paying so much for a hotel. Other people financially support us, so I worry what people will think." She told me the amount she would be spending.

I smiled. Then I said, "First off, I believe it's right and normal to take a break. It's for your mental, emotional, and spiritual health. Think of it as necessary money spent on health, like going to the doctor and getting a much needed prescription."

"Really?" She exhaled. "Thank you."

"But," I said, "my hunch is that this has more to do with worth issues than anything else. Yes, you may be worried about what other people think, but really, it sounds like you're worried about what you think."

"It seems like a lot of money."

"You are worth it," I told her, trying not to laugh at myself because we could certainly be having the same conversation about me. In fact, I know I've had similar interaction with my husband many times when we've faced a financial decision. I'm happy, even joyful-giddy, to give money away to others. But to spend it on myself? Very difficult. I leave thrift stores with guilt, to give you an idea of how much I struggle with this.

Of course, I realize that I live a privileged life compared to most of the world. That one fact also prevents me from enjoying things and money and trips. I feel guilty. Who am I to deserve anything? And what of my brothers and sisters in need? However, if we do have our heads (and wallets) screwed on straight, if we endeavor to live life with an open hand, then we must also afford God the same generosity. He is the God of open hands who lavishes far more on us than we deserve, starting with the indescribable gift of his Son, who gave his life so we could live void of shame and fear. That is lavish giving. And it's directed to the entire human race, including me. And you.

2. God Loves Us Even When We Lack

Who are we to thwart God's generosity? Who are we to declare that our lives are unworthy of blessing? Job declared the truth about God's sovereignty, that his taking away is also balanced with his outrageous generosity. "The LORD gave me what I had, and the LORD has taken it away. Praise the name of the LORD!" (Job 1:21). We must hold both gifts in tandem—the removing, the giving. We must accept both from Jesus, but many of us (me included) wallow only in what we lack, believing that harshness and punishment are the only ways God deals with us—the stern Father always wanting us to live up to expectations, always meting out justice because we're so darn unworthy.

Job's statement can foster two misconceptions if we jump to extremes. One extreme is that God only gives to us, and if we learn to say the right words, he must bless us because we said the right words. The other is that God only takes from us, and if we have anything of worth, it is to be shunned and discarded. One is the health and wealth gospel, the belief that God solely exists to bless us, and the other is asceticism, the avoidance of all worldly pleasures.

But Job uses both phrases. The giving. The taking away. And the response to both. If God blesses us financially, we praise him. If God allows financial stress, we praise him. In all things, as Paul said, we learn the secret of beautiful contentment. And that contentment is tied directly to the fact that we are worthy and loved by God, the perfect parent who knows that children who receive everything they ask for become spoiled but who also loves to lavish gifts on his children.

Consider again Paul's important words, and discern how they echo Job's: "Not that I was ever in need, for I have learned how to be content with whatever I have. I know how to live on almost nothing or with everything. I have learned the secret of living in every situation, whether it is with a full stomach or empty, with plenty or little. For I can do everything through Christ, who gives me strength" (Phil. 4:11–13). We often quote the latter part of those verses, applying them to living a victorious, awesome life, but taken in context, Paul's words take on an entirely new meaning. We can accept financial duress with the strength God supplies. But we can also joyfully receive provision from him (often through the generosity of others) with that same kind of strength.

3. God Solves the Deepest Issues of the Heart— Something Money Cannot Do

We were bought with the price of a life—Jesus Christ's. Therefore, we have value. His life was sacrificed for ours. People value what they pay for. God values what he paid for. Blood for a birthright and a blessing.

Now reflect on Hebrews 11:6: "And without faith it is impossible to please God, because anyone who comes to him must believe that he exists and that he rewards those who earnestly seek him" (NIV).

See that word *impossible*? It hurts to read it. For a majority of my life I thought pleasing God meant doing a bunch of things, being productive. And I honestly didn't think my incessant worry about money meant anything to the Almighty God. I worked hard, hoped for money, and placed my trust firmly in its ability to rescue me.

I trusted money to solve my problems.

I ran to finances first when I wanted freedom from stress.

I remember my friend Paul in Ghana who can't run to money when life knocks him down. He can't go to a doctor when he's sick with malaria (it costs money). He can't buy his way out of trouble. All he can do is run first to God, trusting him as Provider.

Sometimes I am jealous of Paul. He has everything stripped away—no props, no crutches. He has to trust God. I, instead, run to what I feel will fill me. I naively (and sadly) believe in lesser things. Surrounded (and drowning?) in stuff keeps me insulated from trusting him. Aren't we all like this to a certain degree? We wrongly believe that when a certain amount of provision comes our way, then we will stop worrying.

But worrying is a terrible disease. It's cancer. It cannot stop multiplying. If we cannot be grateful and peaceful with what we have right now, we will never be grateful and peaceful with more.

4. God Is the Best Master

I love what Ian Morgan Cron writes in his excellent book *Chasing Francis*. "There is a law in physics that applies to the soul. No two objects can occupy the same space at the same time; one thing must displace another. If your heart's crammed tight with material things and a thirst for wealth, there's no space left for God."[3]

Oh dear.

There the truth is—in black and white. Can't serve two masters. Can't trust two masters.

Money isn't the answer to stress. Jesus is. But often my heart's been so full of my own schemes for provision that I've neglected to trust God for his provision.

So we choose to bow before the cross—the beautiful, terrible cross. That place where our desires are crucified and we are undone, stripped, made bare. Where we realize that we took nothing into this world and will take nothing from it. Money is small. It's a tool for the kingdom, but it is not our savior. It cannot make our hearts right. It cannot ultimately solve our issues, curb our stress, or love us. It simply is.

So make a decision to surrender right now, asking for forgiveness. Choose to shift your heart away from worry, from trusting in money instead of God, from materialism, from striving too hard. Place your gaze on Jesus, the author and finisher of your faith.

5. God Is Bigger than Our Scarcity Mind-Set

Have you battled a scarcity mind-set? I worry I won't have enough—enough money, possessions, food, clothing, you name it. I let my mind automatically turn to sadness when one bad thing happens. I'm more apt to see the glass half empty than half full. I jump to negative conclusions quicker than you can say "Eeyore." It makes me sad that I'm this way. It seems to be ingrained in me, part of my DNA. I see others who are joyfully anticipatory, who seem to smile even when life hurls frustration their way. They acknowledge the pain, dust themselves off, and go on. They choose to believe in abundance even when the pantry is empty.

I'm not talking about a Pollyanna mentality. I once knew a woman who drove me batty. She denied reality when bad things happened and said, "Just choose joy," over and over again. It sounded robotic, rehearsed, inauthentic.

There has to be a middle ground between a scarcity mind-set and a denial of reality. It's about having true joy, effervescent abundance of contentment. And acknowledging the truth about our circumstance but choosing to find something beautiful from the ashes of it.

According to Stephen R. Covey, "People with a scarcity mentality tend to see everything in terms of win-lose. There is only so much; and if someone else has it, that means there will be less for me. The more principle-centered we become, the more we develop an abundance mentality, the more we are genuinely happy for the successes, well-being, achievements, recognition, and good fortune of other people. We believe their success adds to . . . rather than detracts from . . . our lives."[4]

But how do we get there?

This struggle involves retraining the way we think. And that takes conversation. We have to share our thoughts with others. It's in those times that we realize just how dark we've become. And then we remember to review our days, to reframe what has happened so our lives do not seem so scarce. We can do this. Decide right now to say the Abundance Pledge:

1. I'll have an abundant day if I look for blessings rather than deprivations.

2. Instead of pining to be picked, I'll choose to pick someone and make their day joyful.

3. I'll remember that my worth is intangible, not based on tasks accomplished or people's approval but on how deeply Jesus loves me.

4. If something bad happens to me today, I'll choose to silence the voice that says more bad things are inevitable. Instead, I'll view the setback as a means to grow and move forward with hope.

Saying this Abundance Pledge every morning will help your mind snap away from deprivation and scarcity to a wide-eyed anticipation of what's next. I pray the words resonate with you.

6. God, Not Wealth, Strengthens Our Souls

An in-your-face advertisement stared back at me, all the famous people in black and white beckoning me to attend their wealth seminar. One of the seminars was called "Why God Wants You to Be Wealthy." I have much I could say about the topic. Things about the rich young ruler walking away sad because he loved wealth more than obedience, how Jesus said the poor were blessed, how small that eye of the needle is, how narrow the path, and how loving the poor means loving Jesus.

Instead, I'll remind myself of this truth:

> He who is faithful in a very little thing is faithful also in much; and he who is unrighteous in a very little thing is unrighteous also in much. Therefore if you have not been faithful in the use of unrighteous wealth, who will entrust the true riches to you? And if you have not been faithful in the use of that which is another's, who will give you that which is your own? No servant can serve two masters; for either he will hate the one and love the other, or else he will be devoted to one and despise the other. You cannot serve God and wealth.
>
> Luke 16:10–13 NASB

7. God Blesses Our Pursuit of True Riches

What are true riches? Those things that follow us to eternity. The folks with whom we've shared the news of Jesus. The cup of water we've given to the thirsty. The child far away whom we've helped clothe and feed. The sacrifices we've made for the sake of the gospel. These follow us to eternity. An eternal weight of glory, it's called. But there are true riches to be found here on earth as well:

- A heart that forgives even when wronged 491 times
- A soul that's broken; but in all the right ways
- A relationship with Jesus that is rich beyond measure
- A capacity to endure
- An ability to let God be the manager of reputation
- A wealthy prayer life

- A Job-like ability to rejoice in God even when he seems distant
- A disdain for petty gossip, which has been replaced by a desire to bless others with encouraging words
- A longing for justice by God's hands and not one's own

If this is the kind of wealth the smiling lady in the advertisement for the wealth seminar promises in her talks, then sign me up. I want that kind of wealth—both the ability to do works that count for eternity and the hope for a changed, dynamic heart. That's biblical wealth.

How do we find it? Read Scripture. Be faithful when no one sees. Tell the truth. Have integrity. Refuse to praise your glorious self—instead, focus on the One who made you. Manage your earthly wealth in such a way that makes God grin. Give stuff away. Don't get so entangled in acquiring and managing wealth that you walk the sorry road of the rich young ruler. Be satisfied with your lot. Trust that God sees you. Focus on charity to combat greed, for the hallmark of a worthy person's life is unhindered generosity. Rejoice when wealth eludes you. Yes, rejoice. Because life is more than money. People are more important than things.

It's a narrow road. And time is short. Why waste it chasing things that will burn anyway? Why fritter away our lives on things that just don't matter? Why neglect those who starve, those who bleed, those who suffer, while we whine about not having enough money to buy the next greatest thing?

Part of finding our worth is learning to believe that inner whisper of the Holy Spirit—trusting him to order our lives, sing our worth, and provide for us in lean times. Despite your financial state, rejoice. Practice contentment. Life has a plethora of problems—whether you're rich or poor—and God's affection is the same for all his people.

....

TRUTH:
My Worth Is Tied to the Weighty Worth of Jesus.

....

Questions for Reflection or Discussion

1. When have you equated your worth or lack of worth with the amount of money you had? What happened? Why does money have such a sway over how we feel about ourselves?

2. List ten times God has met your needs. Thank him for his beautiful provision.

3. How have you reconciled that God loves you even when you struggle financially? Who in your life has been the most faithful example of trusting God through difficult financial times? What have you learned from them?

4. Why do we tend to believe money can buy us happiness? When have you believed that? What circumstances have caused you to change your mind about the connection between money and happiness?

5. Write out the Abundance Pledge, and then say it out loud. Which truth is most difficult for you right now? What would have been most problematic five years ago?

6. How has a scarcity mind-set sabotaged your trust and faith in Jesus? When have you learned balance between chasing wealth and learning to accept good blessings from God?

7. What does Scripture say about chasing wealth? How can you be wildly generous with your money this week?

—————— **WORTH PRAYER** ——————

Jesus, please forgive me for equating my worth with the money I do or don't have. I want to live for your kingdom, using money as a tool and not a measure of my worth. Teach me. Help me understand that even when I struggle financially, you see my need and have the best in mind for me. I want to live an abundant, joy-filled life, free from preoccupation with money. Deliver me from the world's view of wealth, and make me a generous giver. Free me from a mind-set of scarcity. I want to chase you and your everlasting abundance, not capricious wealth. Amen.

11

I Am a Redemptive Story

LIE:
The Whole of Me Is Flawed.

It's amazing to me that God sees our entire story, from the moment we were two-celled wonders to the hour we pull in our last breath. He is omniscient that way, and he is the best storyteller. Except that we tend to get tangled up in the story and, too often, that means rehashing past pain in a hellish loop.

I have told my story, believed I was the sum of that story, and faithfully executed it—sometimes playing the victim, other times the heroine, but mostly I'm a weak character swung hither and yon by the machinations of the story, feeling helpless to move forward. Paralyzed, really.

We forget God's bigness. We replace that bigness with what seems to be the enormity of our failed story. Or we blame everyone else for its outcome. Or we forget that we have a very real adversary who lurks around every corner of our storyworld, seeking to kill, destroy, and steal from us. And therein lies the challenge for us all. We who want desperately to feel worthy must learn the art of better storytelling, honoring God in his rightful (very strong) place, seeing ourselves as active protagonists, viewing people who love or hate us as image-bearers of God, and understanding exactly who the Father of Lies is.

What is your story? What nuances pepper your narrative? Jim Loehr wrote, "The most important story you will ever tell about yourself is the story you tell to yourself."[1] What kind of story have you told about yourself in the past few years? Months? Days?

Before you finish this chapter, I want you to write one paragraph that summarizes your story. What have you lived? Believed? Identifying the story you tell yourself will uncover the deep-down lie you've believed about yourself.

Let's explore a parable together. It's one you've probably read and heard many times. Instead of two brothers, I'm re-creating the story of the prodigal son as the story of the prodigal daughter. See if you can find yourself here.

The Prodigal Daughter

My father tells me he loves me every single day, but his words seem to garble when they reach their way to my heart. I cannot be loved. I am too flawed, too restless, too hungry for this world. My sister, Sarah, lives frustratingly content here within the four walls of our country home, and she seems to heed Father's words when he says them, takes them in like delicacies to the center of who she is. She is the girl who smiles. I am Rebekah, the girl whose smile hides my thirst for adventure.

The moment I am eighteen, I know exactly what I will do. I will make the request that will break his heart, enrage Sarah, hurt Mother, and set me free to soar. I don't need my father. I certainly don't need my sister or mother. I must make my way in this world, must prove that I can live independently. I need no one.

With downcast eyes, I approach Father, who is crouching in the garden hard at work while Mother is preparing the evening meal. "I want to ask you for something," I say clearly.

"Anything you want, dear Rebekah." He stands and brushes dirt from his work-dirty palms.

"I am not sure you mean that, because what I ask for is big." I take in a few breaths. This will not be easy.

His sea-blue eyes glisten under the light of the afternoon sky. "Anything means anything. What can I grant you? Your own garden perhaps?"

"My inheritance," I say. And I let the words impale him.

"You will receive that upon my death, child. Not sooner."

"When you pass," I say, "it will be too late to do what I need to do. The world is a great big place. There is more to life than tilling, harvesting, praying, existing under the heavy sun." I cross my arms across my chest. I mean this.

We stand like two pillars of salt under the waning sun, resolute and stubborn.

He turns away from me. Takes out a red bandanna from his back pocket, wipes his face, then faces me again. "I cannot control you, nor do I want to," he says. "I will always, always love you. I should tell you one thousand things about this world, about what to avoid, about the foolishness of pride and stubborn strength, but—"

"You are giving advice right now," I say.

"So I am. But as your father, I see no good in you venturing away from my protection. I know what is best for you."

"That is where you are dead wrong." I kick at the dirt. "I want my inheritance." The four words slip from my heart, then my lips. I have deadened myself to his affection, those eyes.

"Rebekah," he sighs. "You will have it tomorrow. But hear me now." He stoops to the ground and pulls a weed from the earth. "If you ever get into trouble in this journey of yours, remember what life is like here. Remember how deeply you are loved. Remember that absolutely nothing you do can mar my affection for you. You can return in whatever state you find yourself in. Do you hear me, dear one?"

"Don't call me that," I say. But I regret the words.

Once the money sits in my palms the next morning, I throw a smile Sarah's way. A look of horror overwhelms her face, but I do not care. I am free. Free to be whatever I want to be. No schedules. No one telling me what to do. No so-called protection. I venture by cab to the city, wearing whatever will make me attractive to men. And that is when life begins its crazy descent. I won't bore you with everything I face on the streets. Initially, I party, living lavishly in penthouses and suites. I have so many friends who love me and spend Father's money alongside me. New clothes elate me. A car keeps me free. Jewelry. Spa treatments. Parties with rich and important people. Mojitos. Cosmos. Then more, more, more of the kind of drugs that make me forget the farm, my father, mother, sister.

Except that some days I elevator to the roof, teeter my way toward the building's vacant edge, and wonder aloud if I made a terrible mistake. The hole I thought would be filled by everything the world offers only gapes wider. The more I try to fill it with the next exciting thing, the emptier I feel after the initial thrill. The stars above my head only insult me, happy in the way they dance in their courses. And they are the same stars my family gazes on, no doubt, while they hate and resent me.

Money buys happiness, some say. But they are wrong. Because money is not infinite. It slips through your hands like beach sand—but unlike the sand, there is no gathering it back. My beauty, too, fades with the loss of the money. The stress of worrying about my next meal emaciates my face and darkens the pads under my eyes. My friends leave as soon as the money is gone, abandoning me on the streets with no means to live.

But even then I know the truth. My father's words cannot be true. He will not welcome me back. He will shun me, disown my sorry self for squandering his precious money. I insulted him to his core when I exited his life, and my actions can never be forgiven. Ever.

So I prostitute myself. The more I playact with sex-hungry men, the more I cement my father's inevitable hatred for me. His daughter—the selfish one, the marred one, the broke and broken one, the dirty one.

But one day I face the reality of who I am like a slow dawning of a dream. I am hungry, so hungry my stomach no longer growls. I am beaten. Under my left eye lives a purple bruise courtesy of my latest trick. I am diseased. And I have no shoes. I dream of farm-fresh meals. Of laughter around the dinner table. Of clean air. Of love.

But I am worthless. Utterly so. I have nothing to show for my time of independent living but scars and sickliness. When I see table scraps in someone's trash and long to eat them (all right, actually I do eat them—roast beef, mashed potatoes, green beans—all cold with pockets of mold), I know it's time to walk my sorry self home. Perhaps Father will hire me to work the fields, to earn back what I've taken. I certainly hope he will. I have an impossible amount of money to pay back, and the people of my hometown will make me adhere to their traditions—particularly the shaming ceremony—in order to return.

I will walk the Main Street of Shame, while townspeople wag their heads. They will smash mason jars full of harvest grains at my feet, a reminder of all I've stolen from them, including their reputation and stature in this world. My mother will embarrass herself by jogging toward me, then kissing me, while Father stews at home, thinking of my punishment. This is simply how these things go.

The journey home is without luxury. I hitchhike my way to the gate of our farm, thank the scary-looking man whose truck I rode in, and stand there, immobilized. I try to smooth my clothes, but they are ragged. On the horizon, I see the town below. I hear the commotion of Main Street. But I don't expect to see him standing on the crest of the closest field.

Father.

He runs at the sight of me. Sprints. He breaks every rule our town has established, and for a moment, I wonder if he is running out of hatred.

I want to turn and run away again. But I am far too weak. So I stand, waiting for the inevitable rebuke. *Oh, look who's back, Miss Adventurer. The one who squanders. Why are you here? Who do you think you are?*

Father's pace doesn't slow. It quickens. I hear his footfalls on the hardened earth, then look at my feet—worn, torn toenails, no shoes. I kneel in the dirt, hoping my humiliation will soften him. I will earn back what I've stolen by toiling in the dust.

But he runs right to me, lifts me from the ground, and wraps me tightly in a hug. "My daughter, my daughter, my daughter," he cries. "You are home. You are home with me, where you should be."

I try to push him away. And for a moment I'm successful.

"Let me look at you, Rebekah," he says. "You are beautiful. My beautiful daughter."

"No, Father, I am not. You are lying to me. I don't deserve your words. I have ruined everything. Wasted your money. Wrecked my life. People have used me up, so much so that I am a hollow woman. Please just hire me. I owe you everything. I can pay you back. The shame is too heavy."

He puts an earth-stained finger to my mouth, hushing me. He takes off his coat, wraps it around me because I am shivering, and says, "My dear, dear daughter. You are found. I have waited on tiptoes, searching the horizon every single day for your return. And here you are."

He throws me a party I do not deserve, but I realize this celebration is not for me. It's a celebration of my father's utter audaciousness, for the sake of his love for me. Townspeople embrace him, tell him he's a saint, and I agree. Sarah pouts before, during, and after the occasion, not gracing the party with her sour presence. I understand why. I am the undeserving one. But Father is steadfast in his love for me and spends the next year restoring me. He tells me I'm beautiful. Says I'm worth more than the ranch, the sky, the wildflowers dotting the horizon. I struggle to believe him, but I am finally beginning to understand.

I once was lost, you see. Completely, helplessly lost. But in the arms of my father, I am settling into living found.

You may read this story and think, *Well, that's not me. I haven't run away. My story is vanilla. I struggle to understand and live in light of God's love, yes, but I haven't squandered my faith. I haven't been wasteful or extravagant. Wild? Not me.*

Perhaps you identify more with Sarah in the following story. Read on . . .

The Pharisee Daughter

I work so hard. Beat myself up to be perfect, acceptable. I am Sarah, the daughter who embodies the word *faithful*. My life is strict and safe, and I spend it for the sake of my family. Life works well in that scenario, wonderfully so. Until my sister shames my father by demanding her inheritance. To be honest, that thought has never entered my mind. I am the good girl who plays by the rules, but Rebekah has always been the one with the insatiable need for more.

When Father gives her the money, I rage inside. How dare he grant such a foolish request. It makes me feel as if I have been an idiot all these years, biding my time, doing the right thing, while my sister simply makes demands and gets the world. I stay in the confines of my life as she skips off to cities we've been warned against. As she leaves the farm, I take a broom and sweep away her dusty footprints. With each swish, I force myself to wipe her from my memory. She is dead to me.

Living at home becomes more duty. The bitterness in my heart at my father's capricious generosity makes my stomach turn. He is often available to me, as is Mother, but I cannot approach them for fear of interrupting their anguish, their endless discussions about their lost daughter. What about me?

I do things. I accomplish. I put my head down and get the work done, joylessly.

The day Rebekah returns, bile rises up into my throat. Instead of the shaming ceremony where our town shouts rightful insults while smashing jars at her feet, cutting deep into her flesh, Father violates all the codes and sprints to greet her. He dignifies her with his cloak, then throws a party, inviting everyone to see what he calls "true reconciliation and love."

But I want none of it. I complain. "Why didn't you give me parties, Father?" I spit.

He rebuffs me with words about Rebekah being lost and now found. How I've always had everything he had to offer but simply didn't ask. While the people shout and laugh and dance in the barn adjacent to our home, I watch from the front window and curse. I am not the special one. I am not the wanted one. I live only to do my duty, build my solitary life, and watch how Father blesses my ungrateful sister.

This, too, may not seem to fit your story. But think a little deeper. Have you ever felt like God loves other people more than he loves you? You check things off your spiritual to-do list, often without his strength, and wonder why you feel so very far from him. You've done everything right—attended the cool Christian women conferences, volunteered in the nursery, spent your life being the good girl—only to find your faith in a lifeless lump. Devoid of the energy and love of Jesus. You see those prodigals with their awesome life-from-death stories, and you envy them.

The truth: their wild stories eventually brought them to the feet of Jesus, but your safe story kept you from him. You've missed Jesus because you've lived the Christian life in your power, your wherewithal. And that is an empty, bitter way to live.

The truth: your story matters just as much as that of your wild sister. The Father who ran to her runs to you. It's a matter of perspective. He has been near you all along, but your need to impress him with your right living has erected a wall between the two of you.

The centrality of all our stories, whether prodigal or plain ol' obedient, is this one crucial thing: desperation. Until we are desperate for the Father, until we dirty our feet walking the many miles home, until we admit our complete need for him, we cannot know the kind of loving, intimate fellowship we desire. The difference between the two women was desperate humility.

One had it.

The other didn't.

I'm indebted to Jared Herd, the former teaching pastor at my church, for opening my eyes to this story afresh and providing some cultural background for understanding it. He shared with me about the *Kezazah* ceremony that took place in first-century Jewish society. In the ceremony, those who had shamed their families and entire community by wasting their money among the Gentiles had to return to their town while people smashed clay pots at their feet, physically illustrating that they had shattered their reputation and were cut off from the community. In this ceremony, the mother was allowed to run to her child and kiss them, but the father stayed back, waiting at home.[2] For a father to run to his estranged son as in the prodigal son story would have been unheard of. A scandal, to be sure. But we know it was an act of absolute indulgent love.

So this story is not really about a rebellious or self-sufficient child. It's about a Father who loves his children so much that he welcomes them home with open arms, no matter their sin, and at the risk of public humiliation. Sound familiar? Remember, Jesus told this parable to the rule-abiding Pharisees, who are illustrated by the older son (for the entire story, check out Luke 15:11–32). He was cautioning them against believing a life of good works made them fit for God's love, while those who were "unholy" were unfit.

We can also see some parallels in the story of Jesus, although he was not a prodigal. He left the comfort of heaven (home), defied all cultural norms (he was supposed to be a political savior, not a religious one), and died on a cross. The party? His resurrection, where he invites everyone—sinner, saint, partier—to his banquet. He embodied what the Jewish people call table fellowship while he walked the earth, dining with the prodigals of the world, much to the angst and anger of the righteous Pharisees.

His story saves our story—in every single way. He is the one standing on tiptoes waiting for our arrival, whether we are returning from a far-off land where we've squandered everything or simply turning from living life "perfectly" in our own strength. The banquet table is open for all to join, and he's written the invitation in his blood.

That's the story of our worth. The story of our dignity. The story of our true wealth in a wealth-warped world. Jesus loves us so much that he sacrificed his life for us. He knew the truth that nothing significant in the kingdom of God happens unless there is sacrifice. So he spent himself—for the wayward, for the "good" ones, for us all.

Jesus said, "There is no greater love than to lay down one's life for one's friends" (John 15:13). He was talking about his love here, his daring to die in our place. It's as if we are pedestrians crossing a busy street and Jesus sees a car careening toward us. Instead of letting us be crumpled by steel and bumpers and tires, he pushes us out of the way and faces the car alone. We are saved. He is not. But his sacrifice grants us life.

We do not need to live in the muck of our sin anymore (prodigal), nor do we need to try to manufacture our story by our own sheer effort (prodigal's sibling). Instead, we can recognize who is the hero of our story (Jesus). And we can slow down enough to hear his grand whispers. He is, indeed, the author after all: "Therefore, since we have so great a cloud of witnesses surrounding us, let us also lay aside every encumbrance and the sin which so easily entangles us, and let us run with endurance the race that is set before us, fixing our eyes on Jesus, the *author* and perfecter of faith, who for the joy set before Him endured the cross, despising the shame, and has sat down at the right hand of the throne of God" (Heb. 12:1–2 NASB, emphasis added).

In light of that, how can we live an amazing story? Here are three ways.

1. Realize That God Uses Flawed Heroes

I used to think that for God to use me, I had to be perfect. I figured God wanted flawless folks to represent him on earth. One particular favorite quote of mine has helped me see how faulty my thinking was.

> Christian perfection is not, and never can be, human perfection. Christian perfection is the perfection of a relationship to God which shows itself amid the irrelevancies of human life. When you obey the call of Jesus Christ, the first thing that strikes you is the irrelevancy of the things you have to do, and the next thing that strikes you is the fact that other people seem to be living perfectly consistent lives. Such lives are apt to leave you with the idea that God is unnecessary, by human effort and devotion we can reach the standard God wants. In a fallen world this can never be done. I am called to live in perfect relation to God so that my life produces a longing after God in other lives, not admiration for myself. Thoughts about myself hinder my usefulness to God. God is not after perfecting me to be a specimen in His showroom; He is getting me to the place where He can use me. Let Him do what He likes.[3]

Truth: the editor makes the story sing.

Truth: great stories have conflict.

Truth: the author gets the glory for the story.

2. Let Go of Drama Trauma

Some people need to have trauma define them; they thrive on the drama of trauma. Of course it's easier to see that trait in others. We can discern, after a series of interactions with someone, if they are addicted to drama and need to be in crisis, then rescued to feel alive. Oh, so easy. It's easy for me to see how someone can form their entire identity from being a victim.

190

Funny how I can point things out in others (specks) when I can't see them in myself (logs). Here's the thing: I have reveled in my victim status. I have gained much empathy by sharing my stories, by talking frankly about my struggles. While I do believe the body of Christ should err more on the side of authentic disclosure, there is a line I sometimes cross. If I am telling you my issues for the sake of gaining your empathy, it's an empty pursuit. My fulfillment must come not from your sweet empathy but from being Jesus's beloved daughter. If I am relying on others to fill up my holes, then I'll surely leak. If I do things to emphasize my drama-queen ways, I'm settling for a shallow hope—that someone will take notice and say, "Oh yeah, that's really hard." Where does that leave me? Sure, I now have someone who feels sad alongside me. But I haven't changed, and I'm left with an empty heart.

What do we need to do? Slay the drama queen.

- Dare to run to Jesus when we want to gather a passel of folks around us to rescue, cheer for, and empathize with us. Go to him *first*, not last.
- Dare to believe that we are okay, even if we're not telling all our painful stories.
- Dare to trust that God is bigger than our particular trauma, and he will walk us through the pain in his perfect timing.
- Dare to stop managing our image and let God have the glory.
- Dare to be quiet, even when it means our reputation could get tarnished.
- Dare to first empathize with others instead of internally demanding everyone empathize with us.
- Dare to stop playing the victim.

It's a painful lesson. Part of the way I believe God has helped me cope with my difficult childhood is by giving me the ability to process what happened out loud. But perhaps that was a gift for childhood, and now that I'm an adult, I need to learn a new way of coping—to run headlong to him first, process with him initially, then invite others into the circle after he has profoundly met me in my pursuit.

3. Be Careful with Other People's Stories

Have you ever had days when you have felt the weight of the world's stories? When you've heard about too many awful things people do to one another and wondered where God is and why he doesn't just fix this mess of a world? Sometimes all these stories make me want to pull my hair out. Other times I just want to cry. Life should not be like this—with these stories of abuse. Perhaps you have one too?

People should not worship money and discard people.

They should not satisfy their sexual urges by abusing the vulnerable, helpless, and unsuspecting.

They should not defraud the weak because they see them as a source of easy income.

They should not abandon families.

Hearing these stories, whether face-to-face or via news feeds or from emails, nearly breaks me. I feel responsible, somehow, to fix, to make right, to bring justice. And all the while, my shoulders simultaneously sag and tense. Sag from the enormity of the abuse. Tense from my inability to right the wrongs. *This is wrong,* I think. *Maybe God put me here to stand up for people who can't find their voices. Maybe I'm supposed to be one of the ones who says, "No more!" Maybe.*

Or maybe I'll just cocoon myself away, rocking under the weight of stories, immobilized by sadness.

We can't bear this weight.

Not by ourselves. Not in our supposed strength. We are weak. We are needy. We are helpless to fix the mess, the pain, the anguish.

In times like these, we can either flee or run to Jesus. With honesty. With frailty. With so little to offer except our willingness. Consider Jesus on that cross, how he bore the weight of all the sad stories. He is the sin-bearer and the pain-bearer, shouldering the sins we've all committed and the damage the sins have created. He suffered the evil, the mocking, the jeering, the abuse—for us.

It may not seem like life is fair.

It may not seem like justice will ever prevail in other people's stories, or even our own.

For the sexually abused who share their stories and are dismissed or not believed or ridiculed or silenced or told to "get over it."

For the spouse in an abusive marriage, not knowing where to turn, lacking volition due to years of psychological and physical torment.

For the child who wants to be wanted yet remains abandoned.

For the trafficked victim, enslaved and without hope or a voice.

For the one who has been stolen from, defrauded, perpetrated against.

There aren't simple answers to these issues. You can't put a Christian cliché Band-Aid on them and hope people will suddenly become resilient. When something has been stolen from someone, it takes years to find renewal, redemption. Undoing all the taking takes time. Which is where we come in as story-bearers. By the strength of Jesus, we choose to light up that which has been lurking in the dark. We decide to no longer let these atrocities happen on our watch. We choose to shoulder the pain of the one who cries that she can't "get over it."

We listen.

We pray.

We advocate.

We stand in the gap between pat answers and genuine help. Not as vigilantes but as fellow sufferers.

But then we do something necessary and brave: when we get overwhelmed and tired, and the stories weigh us down, we gently hand them to Jesus for safekeeping, remembering that he is the One who sees and shoulders every story and will someday right the seemingly wrong endings.

I'm writing this in the quietness of night. Another email slips through to me—another weighty story with a hint of blame that I seem to be okay while others suffer. I let the words sink in. I feel their heaviness as I type in the dark. I try not to cry.

Like you, I am one small person on a big, big planet who simply wants to say this: you are not alone. Your story matters.

What story do you want to live today? I'm less interested in living a triumphal story and more determined to live an authentic one that acknowledges life's conflicts, confusion, and pain, as well as God's presence. I remember that, as a writer, the best stories have pain before growth, conflict before resolution, and suspense before the denouement. We are living a beautiful drama right now. Villains come and go. The plot twists throw us for crazy loops. Enemies become friends, and friends become turncoats. Some loved ones walk away. Others die. Our health is amazing, then failing.

We limp.

We fall.

We get up again.

Because this, our great redemptive story, can be told only if we are protagonists in it, heroically taking the next step through the strength God supplies.

And when we reach heaven's shores, and the end is written on our earthly tale, we'll never regret living a worthy life for Jesus.

That will be when our true story begins, and, finally, we will truly and deeply know our worth.

....

T R U T H :

God Is the Author and Editor of My Story, and He Is Well Pleased with Me as the Protagonist.

....

Questions for Reflection or Discussion

1. What story have you told yourself or about yourself most of your life? What new story would you like to live? How do they differ?

2. What aspects of the prodigal daughter story resonated with you? Why?

3. What part of the Pharisee daughter did you identify with? Why?

4. Whom do you know who is living an amazing, audacious story? How does that encourage you to live differently?

5. How are you a flawed hero? And how does knowing God uses flawed heroes to write history encourage you? (Consider many heroes of the Bible who sinned—Abraham, Moses, David, Rahab, Peter—yet God used them in the most important story ever told.)

6. Have you ever succumbed to drama trauma? How has that hurt your perception of the situation you were in? Who in your life suffers from drama trauma? Who is the antithesis of drama? What can you learn from both people?

7. How can you encourage another person's story this week? When has someone encouraged you to live a better story?

WORTH PRAYER

Jesus, I want to live the story you have for me. Forgive me for settling for lesser things or thinking my flaws relegate me to an awful story. No, instead, help me see your hand in the midst of my mayhem. I need to understand your love for me whether I rebel or obey. Please help me find that place of desperation where I make you the hero of my story and go solely to you to meet my needs. Help me create a drama-free home, and give me the insight I need to discern other people's stories and cheerlead them toward their climax and denouement. Amen.

Conclusion

I Am Living a Life Worth Living

People have two lives—one where they wander around searching for worth and an incredible one after they discover it.

Caitlin Muir

I sat in the living room thinking about this book. I turned to a friend and asked what he thought about worth. His response? "Don't you think God favors some over others?" he asked.

His question startled me. I'd always believed all of us had equal worth as image-bearers of God. I knew he hailed from a different theological perspective than I did, but I didn't expect he'd make this conclusion. He said something like, "I mean, don't you think he assigns more worth to the people he's chosen before the foundation of the world than the ones chosen for damnation? It seems in this instance, some are worth more than others."

I didn't respond in the moment. We weren't having an argument, and neither of us spoke in adversarial tones. I needed to think about his words a bit. Are some of us worth more than others? As I thought about it further, I had to return to the pivotal point of history where Jesus shed his own privilege and paid the price we could not pay. He paid for humanity, for all of us. For terrorists and toddlers. For Hitlers and Mother Teresas. For the indifferent and the passionate. For me and for you. Worth, as I've mentioned throughout this book, is a term of weight, of measure, of money. Our worth is based not on our intrinsic value per se but on the invaluable work of Jesus Christ on our behalf. If only we could grasp that!

Simply put: it's not about you or me conjuring our worth. It's about Jesus settling it. Once and for all. No matter how you feel at this very moment, reading words plain on the page. It is not dependent on you. Perfect you. Imperfect you. Bumbling you. Sweet you. Nor is it tied to length of days. Whether you've followed Jesus for eighty years or eighty minutes, your worth is assured. He's got you. He holds you. He keeps you in relationship with him. Your worth is a known, provable fact because of Jesus's audacious act on the cross. It's the truth you can base your life on, thanks to the beautiful resurrection. And if you could rest there in that place of worth, oh the peace you would revel in.

That's my deep desire for you as you close the pages of this book. May you look at yourself in the mirror and genuinely smile at who you see—a woman dearly loved by Jesus, one worth sacrificing for, being gentle with. If this still feels difficult, you might try following Brandi Luiz's lead. "In my devotion corner, I have a handwritten note saying, 'How lovely is your dwelling place, O Lord Almighty!' (Ps. 84:1 NIV) followed by the words, 'I am lovely.' I look at it every morning and remind myself that I am loved by the Almighty."[1]

You are his lovely dwelling place, infused with worth.

Even when you walk with a limp.

Even when you feel unloved.

Even when you're overlooked.

Even when you overwork to prove your worth.

Even when your strength ebbs and fades.

Even when insecurity takes deep root.

Even when you feel ugly.

Even when the past strangles you.

Even when nothing you do seems to matter.

Even when money and success elude you.

Even when your story takes violent turns.

You are living a life worth living.

The God who made the sparkling stars loves you affectionately. He delights in you. Let your worth rest there. Joy and freedom will, no doubt, follow.

Notes

Chapter 1 The Lie I Believed

1. Dorothy Sayers, *The Mind of the Maker* (New York: Continuum, 2005), 129.

Chapter 2 I Am Wildly Loved

1. See John 14:6.
2. Mark Buchanan, *The Rest of God* (Nashville: Thomas Nelson, 2006), 7.
3. Len Sweet, Twitter post, October 10, 2014, 6:48 a.m., https://twitter.com/lensweet/status/520571553696972800.
4. Cloud, *Necessary Endings* (Grand Rapids: Zondervan, 2011), 133.
5. There are books written about this difficult process. I highly recommend Henry Cloud and John Townsend, *Boundaries: When to Say Yes, How to Say No to Take Control of Your Life* (Grand Rapids: Zondervan, 1992).
6. Cloud, *Necessary Endings*, 139.
7. Jon Weece, *Jesus Prom: Life Gets Fun When You Love People Like God Does* (Nashville: Thomas Nelson, 2014), 7.

Chapter 3 I Am More than a To-Do List

1. Liz Wolf, email to author, October 6, 2014.
2. Katherine Reay, *Lizzy and Jane* (Nashville: Thomas Nelson, 2014), 304.
3. L. B. Cowman, *Streams in the Desert* (Grand Rapids: Zondervan, 1996), 336.
4. Jim Loehr, *The Power of Story: Change Your Story, Change Your Destiny in Business and in Life* (New York: Free Press, 2008), 136.
5. Ibid., 28, 52.
6. Tim Hansel, *You Gotta Keep Dancing* (Colorado Springs: David C. Cook, 1985), 142.

Notes

Chapter 4 I Am Uncaged

1. Sarah Van Diest, email to author, September 16, 2014.

Chapter 5 I Am Weakly Strong

1. Sue Keddy, *Life without Jim* (Sisters, OR: Deep River, 2014), 18.
2. Ibid., 51.
3. Tim Hansel, "You Gotta Keep Dancin'," (Colorado Springs: David C. Cook, 1985), 143.
4. Ema McKinley and Cheryl Ricker, *Rush of Heaven* (Grand Rapids: Zondervan, 2014), 229.
5. I also share this story in my memoir, *Thin Places*.
6. Hansel, *You Gotta Keep Dancing*, 43.
7. Bob Goff, *Love Does* (Nashville: Thomas Nelson, 2014), 9.
8. Cowman, *Streams*, 147.

Chapter 6 I Am Secure

1. Hansel, *You Gotta Keep Dancing*, 44.
2. Sarah Van Diest, email to author, September 16, 2014.
3. Francis Frangipane, *The Stronghold of God* (Lake Mary, FL: Charisma House, 1998), 107.
4. Ibid., 119.
5. Ibid., 111.
6. Ibid.
7. Trina Traster, "My Husband and I Made It Our Life's Work to Heal Our Daughter," *Redbook*, May 1, 2014, http://www.redbookmag.com/kids-family/advice/reactive-attachment-disorder.

Chapter 7 I Am Beautiful

1. Steve Maraboli, *Unapologetically You: Reflections on Life and the Human Experience* (Port Washington, NY: A Better Today, 2013), 52.
2. Lore Ferguson, "Beautiful beyond Our Control," Hermeneutics, ChristianityToday.com, October 27, 2014, http://www.christianitytoday.com/women/2014/october/beautiful-beyond-our-control.html?paging=off.
3. Ibid.
4. Ibid.

Chapter 8 I Am Chosen

1. This is from the Babylonian Talmud, the section called Sanhedrin, on page 38a.

Chapter 9 I Am Destined for Impact

1. Mike Smith, *The Secret* (Protea Publishing, 2002), 122.
2. Frederick Buechner, *Wishful Thinking: A Seeker's ABC* (San Francisco: HarperOne, 1993).

3. George J. Borjas and Kirk B. Doran, "Prizes and Productivity: How Winning the Fields Medal Affects Scientific Output" (working paper, University of Notre Dame, 2013), 2, http://www3.nd.edu/~tjohns20/RePEc/deendus/wpaper /022_Fields.pdf.

4. Sarah Van Diest, email to author, September 16, 2014.

5. Randy Alcorn, "In What Sense Will Believers Be Judged in Heaven?" Eternal Perspective Ministries, March 28, 2010, http://www.epm.org/resources/2010/ Mar/28/what-sense-will-believers-be-judged-heaven/.

6. Adam Grant, *Give and Take: A Revolutionary Approach to Success* (New York: Viking, 2013), 157.

7. Interview by author: http://www.marydemuth.com/give-and-take/.

Chapter 10 I Am Worth More than a Paycheck

1. Bible Study Tools, s.v. "axios," accessed September 21, 2015, http://www .biblestudytools.com/lexicons/greek/nas/axios.html.

2. Grant, *Give and Take*, 168.

3. Ian Morgan Cron, *Chasing Francis* (Grand Rapids: Zondervan, 2013), 165.

4. http://www.doonething.org/quotes/abundance-quotes.htm.

Chapter 11 I Am a Redemptive Story

1. Loehr, *Power of Story*, 14.

2. See also this informative article: http://deforestlondon.wordpress.com/2010/ 03/14/a-palestinian-perspective-on-the-prodigal-son/.

3. Oswald Chambers, *My Utmost for His Highest* (Westwood, NJ: Barbour and Company, 1963), 337.

Conclusion I Am Living a Life Worth Living

1. Liz Curtis Higgs, "Your 50 Favorite Proverbs: #16 What Will People Think?" accessed September 23, 2015, http://www.lizcurtishiggs.com/your-50-favorite -proverbs-16-what-will-people-think/?replytocom=96781-respond.

Mary DeMuth is a former church planter in France and the author of more than thirty books. A sought-after international speaker, she has overcome (through Jesus's healing) a difficult past to become an authentic example of what it means to live a brand-new story. She lives in Texas with her family.

Follow Speaker and Blogger

MARY DeMUTH

Blog: marydemuth.com

facebook.com/AuthorMaryDeMuth

@MaryDeMuth

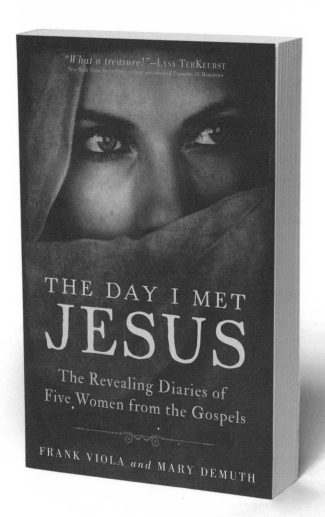

THE DAY I MET

JESUS

The Revealing Diaries of
Five Women from the Gospels

FRANK VIOLA and MARY DEMUTH

"What a treasure!"—LYSA TERKEURST
New York Times bestselling author, president of Proverbs 31 Ministries

"What a treasure! The way Mary and Frank portray their stories
will help any woman who has experienced heartbreak, loneliness,
and rejection step right into the extravagant grace and love of Jesus."

—**Lysa TerKeurst**,

New York Times bestselling author of *The Best Yes*; president of Proverbs 31 Ministries

BakerBooks
a division of Baker Publishing Group
www.BakerBooks.com

 Available wherever books and ebooks are sold.

LIKE THIS
BOOK?
Consider sharing it with others!

- Share or mention the book on your social media platforms. Use the hashtag **#WorthLiving**.

- Write a book review on your blog or on a retailer site.

- Pick up a copy for friends, family, or strangers! Anyone who you think would enjoy and be challenged by its message.

- Share this message on Twitter or Facebook. "**I loved #WorthLiving by @MaryDeMuth //@ReadBakerBooks**"

- Recommend this book for your church, workplace, book club, or class.

- Follow Baker Books on social media and tell us what you like.

 Facebook.com/ReadBakerBooks

 @ReadBakerBooks